YOU
MATTER
to GOD

Books by Derek Prince

Biography

Appointment in Jerusalem
Derek Prince: A Biography by Stephen Mansfield

Guides to the Life of Faith

Blessing or Curse: You Can Choose
Bought with Blood
Declaring God's Word
The End of Life's Journey
Faith to Live By
God Is a Matchmaker
God's Remedy for Rejection
The Grace of Yielding
How to Fast Successfully
Husbands and Fathers
Marriage Covenant
Power in the Name
Prophetic Guide to the End Times
Rediscovering God's Church
Rules of Engagement
Secrets of a Prayer Warrior
Shaping History through Prayer and Fasting
Spiritual Warfare
They Shall Expel Demons
Through the Psalms with Derek Prince
Transformed for Life
War in Heaven

Systematic Bible Exposition

Entering the Presence of God
Foundational Truths for Christian Living
Lucifer Exposed
Promised Land
Self-Study Bible Course
You Shall Receive Power

YOU MATTER TO GOD

Discovering Your True Value and Identity in God's Eyes

Derek Prince

Chosen

a division of Baker Publishing Group
Grand Rapids, Michigan

© 2010 by Derek Prince Ministries–International

Published by Chosen Books
a division of Baker Publishing Group
P.O. Box 6287, Grand Rapids, MI 49516-6287
www.chosenbooks.com

Printed in the United States of America

Library of Congress Cataloging-in-Publication Data
Prince, Derek.
    You matter to God : discovering your true value and identity in God's eyes / Derek Prince.
        p.   cm.
    "Compiled from the extensive archives of Derek Prince's unpublished materials and edited by the Derek Prince Ministries editorial team"—T.p. verso.
    ISBN 978-0-8007-9488-0 (pbk.)
    1. Identity (Psychology)—Religious aspects—Christianity. 2. Theological anthropology—Christianity. I. Derek Prince Ministries. II. Title.
    BV4509.5.P753 2010
    248.4—dc22   2009043221

This book was compiled from the extensive archives of Derek Prince's unpublished materials and edited by the Derek Prince Ministries editorial team.

10   11   12   13   14   15   16   7   6   5   4   3   2   1

Contents

Introduction

In the years leading up to Derek Prince's passing at the age of 88, it seems that this amazing Bible teacher became more and more tenderhearted. Not that he had ever lacked compassion. His kindness was evident throughout his life. But if you listen to messages recorded in Derek's later years, you will hear distinct moments when his voice cracked more readily and he choked with emotion—especially when he was sharing about God's goodness and faithfulness.

It seemed that as Derek got closer to the time when he would meet the Lord face to face, he was being tenderized by God. And the topics he shared on later in his life showed it. His emphasis on caring for people—especially widows, orphans and the poor—reflected this softening process. But probably one of the most striking evidences of his increasingly compassionate heart was his teaching on how precious each person is in the sight of God our Father.

Do You Realize How Valuable You Are?

Although Derek remained rock solid as always in his devotion to God's Word and his insistence on its truth and application in every area of life, the gentle element appeared more and more in his teachings—those tender moments when he focused on our value to God. One of the clearest examples was Derek's signature message "Do You Realize How Valuable You Are?"

Much of that material makes up the backbone of this book. We are grateful that *You Matter to God* is placing these life-changing truths in your hands. We hope you will be joining the countless company of people who testify that their lives have been forever helped by this affirming word from Derek Prince.

We do not know all the reasons for this emphasis by Derek on our value to the Lord. Possibly with his decades-long involvement in the ministry of deliverance and spiritual warfare, he saw the horrific damage wrought in people's lives by our mortal enemy, the "accuser of the brethren."

Those ravages of rejection and denunciation prompted Derek to speak greater words of biblical encouragement—in fact, to help people declare scriptural truths to counteract Satan's malignant work of accusation. It was almost as if Derek was mad at hell, and he was not going to take it anymore. Nor did he intend to allow anyone in his worldwide audience to sit still for such brutalization at the hands of the devil.

That is a good thought to keep in mind as you read this book. For it is not only an affirmation of our value to the Father—that you are so valuable to Him that He sent Jesus, His dear Son, to redeem you!—but it is a call to battle. We are joining Derek and calling for you to rise up and say to the one continuously planting accusing thoughts and self-doubt, "The Lord rebuke you!" (see Jude 3:9).

How Do the Books Keep Coming?

Now to address any questions that arise from the phenomenon of another book from Derek Prince, years after he has passed from this earth. People ask us regularly, "How are you able to release a new book even though Derek is no longer with us?" That is a fair question, and the answer is an encouragement.

While he was on earth, Derek was a prolific Bible teacher. In fact, if you were having a conversation with him, he would inevitably begin to share some new insight he was seeing in the Word of God. Most of Derek's teaching occasions were recorded or captured in some form. His archives are full to overflowing. In addition, offices and workers of Derek Prince Ministries around the world continue to come upon previously undiscovered teaching material. One of the DPM offices recently explored a cache of reel-to-reel tapes by Derek and found that these tapes contained teaching sessions not previously known about.

In addition, much of Derek's teaching material that we are already aware of needs to appear in printed form. The bottom line: You can expect to see more books by Derek Prince being released, for many years to come.

We would not even venture to release this material were it not for at least three significant reasons. First is a strong conviction that in these challenging days, the Church desperately needs the kind of substantive teaching Derek offered. A concern for biblical depth was, in fact, one of the main reasons he taught as he did.

Second, Derek's teaching seems to have a timeless quality. Because he focused so determinedly on teaching the Word of God with little embellishment, his teaching carries an eternal quality that transcends contemporary circumstances and issues. Some of Derek's teaching from thirty years ago applies in a more timely way now, if possible, than when he first delivered it.

Third, and possibly most important, the Holy Spirit uses the teaching to make an impact on our lives today. Simply stated, it carries the anointing of the Holy Spirit. Repeatedly we hear from readers that the Lord has used words Derek spoke five, ten or twenty years ago to bring conviction in the present, prompting life-changing direction, course correction and consequent change.

Frankly, as long as Derek's material in any form prompts that kind of Spirit-led response in people's lives, we will continue to make sure it gets into the hands of people all over the world.

And now you hold this type of powerful teaching by Derek Prince in your hands. Our prayer for you is that as you read, you will experience all three of the phenomena we mention above. As you explore this tender, loving work originated by Derek Prince, may the truths you read help you to know deep in your heart how precious you are to the One who created you. And may these truths stir a deep conviction in you to stand boldly in the face of the enemy who accuses you continually, and to oppose him with a deep conviction born out of one simple truth: You know that *you matter to God*.

The International Publishing Team of Derek Prince Ministries

1

Do You Realize How Valuable You Are?

> We have known and believed the love that God
> has for us. God is love, and he who abides in love
> abides in God, and God in him.
>
> 1 John 4.16

We open this book with a question: *Do you realize
how valuable you are?*

I suspect that most of us do not. I would say,
in fact, that one of the prevailing weaknesses of Christians
is a poor sense of self-esteem. Have you noticed this? Some
people never look you fully in the face when you talk to them.
They keep their heads bowed and their eyes never make contact. Others show poor self-esteem in the way they dress. We
know that clothing gives a message that is either positive or
negative. It is never neutral. When I see a young girl in baggy,
loose clothing that leaves no way to know what her form is,

I say to myself, *That is a case of poor self-esteem.* There are many other ways that poor self-esteem reveals itself. I believe it is a common religious problem.

Sometimes we misinterpret this lack of pride as humility, but if you have a poor sense of self-worth, you cannot be humble since you have nothing to be humble about. When you know your own value, then you can walk that narrow road between pride and false humility.

As we examine throughout this book the theme of our value—"What is my importance to God?"—we will find that we are simultaneously discovering the answer to the question of our identity—"Who am I?" God wants us to know who we are. He wants us to know how much we matter to Him.

Our exploration begins with God's original purpose in creating mankind as it is recorded in the opening chapters of Genesis. We will discover as we look into God's Word together throughout this book that His future plans for us only get more and more exciting.

But first, let's look at what Scripture says about how and why God created us the way He did.

The Danger of Pride

I want to remind you of the fact that the creation of Adam and Eve was somewhat down the program in God's creative works. God had already designed a glorious host of angelic beings—seraphim and cherubim and archangels and angels and many other wondrous entities. One of these was one of the chief archangels whose name originally was Lucifer; it was changed to Satan after his rebellion. *Lucifer* means "the bright, the brilliant, the shining one." *Satan* means "the adversary, the enemy." And the reason Lucifer fell was pride.

The most dangerous sin by far that ever threatens us is pride. It is a disastrous sin, and we are all vulnerable to it in one way or another. It does not take much in the way of success for any of us to be easily taken over by pride. In fact, I have seen many ministries ruined this way. My personal prayer is: *Lord, by whatever means is necessary, keep me from becoming proud.*

Now Lucifer rebelled because he was proud, and he had a lot to be proud of. If you are familiar with Ezekiel 28, you may know that it describes two persons. The first half of the chapter deals with the prince of Tyre, and the second half deals with the king of Tyre. The prince of Tyre was a human ruler, but the phrase *king of Tyre* refers to an archangel, the one who was Lucifer. This is how he is described:

> "Thus says the Lord GOD: 'You were the seal of perfection, full of wisdom and perfect in beauty. You were in Eden, the garden of God; every precious stone was your covering: the sardius, topaz, and diamond, beryl, onyx, and jasper, sapphire, turquoise, and emerald with gold. The workmanship of your timbrels and pipes was prepared for you on the day you were created.'"
>
> Ezekiel 28:12–13

Lucifer was a most glorious being. In addition he occupied a place of singular honor. The next verse, which continues below, states: "You were the anointed cherub who covers"—that is, he was the one who covered the throne of God. One cherub was set apart to stretch out his wings over the throne. That honor was given to Lucifer.

> "You were the anointed cherub who covers; I established you; you were on the holy mountain of God; you walked back and forth in the midst of fiery stones. You were perfect in your ways from the day you were created, till iniquity was found in you."
>
> verses 14–15

So here was a glorious heavenly being of inexpressible wisdom, majesty and power who had the singular privilege of covering the throne of God. And yet iniquity was found in him. He grew proud and that pride led to his downfall. He was cast out from the heaven of God into a lower region.

Man Enters the Picture

In our imagination we might picture the three Persons of the Godhead taking counsel together about this event and its implications for the act of man's creation. I spent a good part of my life in Africa, and that caused me to think like an African in many ways, which is to say I picture things very vividly. So I imagine the Godhead discussing this process in this way: "The problem with Lucifer was he was too glori-ous; he was too beautiful; he was too powerful; he was too wise. So let's start at the opposite end. Let's take something so humble and so insignificant that he can never become proud. We'll take some dust. Just dust. Mix it with a little water, make some clay and mold it into a body."

And there it was—the body, formed by God. A perfect body. But it was just clay.

Here is where we begin to discover something remarkable about ourselves. We begin to see the immense value God put on this wonderful creation that He formed of dust: "God said, 'Let Us make man in Our image, according to Our likeness'" (Genesis 1:26).

God is speaking about Himself in the plural, which occurs several times in Scripture. This speaks of the mystery that God is triune, meaning three, yet one. But here is the thing: Just as the Bible reveals the triune nature of God as Father, Son and Spirit (three Persons, yet one God), so the Bible reveals the triune nature of man (three elements, yet one human personality). We will look at how this happened by the breath of God in the next section, and we will explore this aspect of human nature extensively throughout the book, but for now notice that the triune God created a triune man.

Notice also the use of the two words *likeness* and *image*. *Likeness* describes that triune nature of man. The Hebrew word for *image* refers to something entirely different. It recurs in a different form in modern Hebrew in the phrase "to take a photograph." *Image* describes the outward representation. Something in the outward appearance of man, his *image*, represented God.

Some people find that hard to accept. Let me suggest that it was appropriate when God was made manifest in the flesh to come in the form of a male human being, not in the form of an ox or a beetle or a bird. There was something about the outward appearance of the man and woman that could receive the inward form of God.

Then God goes on to say:

"Let them have dominion over the fish of the sea, over the birds of the air, and over the cattle, over all the earth and over every creeping thing that creeps on the earth." So God created man in His own image [we come to the singular here: *His own image*]; in the image of God He created him; male and female He created them.

Genesis 1:26–27

That last phrase is very important. A lot of controversy has been voiced about that particular theme over the years. God created two kinds of persons: male and female. They are quite distinct, and there is nothing in between.

Also, God created them to rule over all the earth. They were God's vice regents.

I was born in India, and at that time there was a vice regent of India who represented the monarch in Britain. That was the position that God planned for the male and female. They

15

would be His vice regents, the viceroys, the ones who reigned on behalf of God Himself. That was God's plan and God's intent for His creation.

How the Man Became a Living Soul

As we look at the record of God creating man, we might find it marvelous that the Bible describes this immensely significant event in one comparatively brief verse. This verse contains such a wealth of riches that we could expatiate on it for a long time. This is how man's creation came about: "And the LORD God formed man of the dust of the ground, and breathed into his nostrils the breath of life; and man became a living being" (Genesis 2:7).

Actually I object to the word *being* used here and in a number of modern translations; I much prefer the word *soul*, which appears in the original King James Version. Man became a living soul.

The Hebrew for the words *the Lord God formed* uses the verb from which the word *potter* is derived. It suggests molding in clay. Although Scripture says that God used *dust*, the verse before this one says "a mist went up from the earth and watered the whole face of the ground" (verse 6). So God was not working with dry dust. It was damp dust. It was moldable clay.

With his humble beginning achieved, man then underwent an astonishing turn. Scripture says that the Lord breathed into his nostrils the breath of life, and man became a living soul. The Spirit of God, the inbreathed breath of God, came into the clay. For me, this is profoundly dramatic and intensely vivid. I am naïve enough to believe it happened the way it is described. If you have problems with that, at least be indulgent with me.

I believe that the Lord God is the Person who was revealed subsequently in human history as Jesus of Nazareth. This is true because, as John says at the beginning of his gospel, all things were made by Him and without Him was not anything made that was made. So Jesus was, if I may say so, the agent of God the Father in this creative process.

One of the interesting aspects of God's dealings with mankind is that every time He does so, He has to stoop. In Creation, then, as I picture it, this wonderful, glorious, divine being knelt down, put His divine hands in the clay and molded a body. It was the most perfect piece of molding that has ever been seen—much greater than anything the greatest artists living on this earth could ever produce. But it was just lifeless; it was just clay.

Then this divine being stooped further and put His divine lips against the lips of clay. He put His divine nostrils against the nostrils of clay, and the Scripture says the Lord "*breathed* into his nostrils the breath of life." I relate that word *breathed* with emphasis because the Hebrew word is a powerfully descriptive word.

Hebrew is a very vivid language. The sound of the words is related to the action they describe. Where it says, "He breathed," in Hebrew it says *napach*. Phonetically the *p* sound in that word is plosive, and it is followed by a prolonged *ch* sound. If you are familiar with phonetics, you know that a plosive is a letter that requires an "explosion" to make it. English has only one good plosive letter, which is *p*. If you say the word *pepper*, for instance, you will see that each *p* is a little explosion.

Then there is the *ch* sound, which no ordinary English-speaking person can say (except for the Scots, who can say it in such words as *loch*). It is a sound missing from our English vocabulary. It is a long, breathed-out, drawn-out sound that contains a sense of dynamic energy.

So when God breathed into man, there was first an explosion and then a long, outgoing breath. In other words, God did not just breathe languidly into that body of clay. He breathed Himself into it. He imparted Himself. Through that breath God came in, and that piece of clay was marvelously, miraculously transformed into a living human body. It became a human person with all the faculties that you and I enjoy. The brain, the heart, the lungs—every organ started to function.

Doctors tell us one human eye has more than three million working parts. If you can believe that happened by accident, you can believe things I cannot! I have no doubt that the mind of God was breathed into that clay and directed the clay to become what God intended it to be. And so, out of that breath came a living human being.

Because of our origin, I believe we have an eternal, divine destiny. That light in us cannot die; it is the light of God. This a solemn thought for all of us because it means we will never cease to exist. We have, therefore, only two alternatives: We can exist in the presence of God, or we can exist in eternal banishment from the presence of God. Each one of us is going to experience one or the other of those choices. We are eternal—for better or for worse.

The Tables Start to Turn

That is our origin. That is where we came from. Do you begin to see that you hold a special place in all of God's created world? The materials of our beginning may have been humble, but we were formed and molded by the hand of God and then inbreathed by the very breath—the Spirit—of God.

If we do not fully realize the implications of this truth, we will never find fulfillment. If we do not realize how inexpressibly valuable we are to God, we can never become what He intends us to become.

Granted we have mistreated this divine workmanship, we have failed to appreciate it, we have squandered God's amazing creation in unrighteous living, in foolish enjoyments and in sinful pleasures, but we are still made in the likeness and image of God.

It should not be surprising, therefore, to find that Satan, now banished from his glorious position, looked on this created being with malicious hatred. He waited for the right time to try to destroy this divine workmanship. Then one day in the Garden, his opportunity came. That is the subject of our next chapter.

2

Missing Our Destiny

So will My word be which goes forth from My mouth; it will not return to Me empty, without accomplishing what I desire, and without succeeding in the matter for which I sent it. . . . Instead of the thorn bush the cypress will come up, and instead of the nettle the myrtle will come up, and it will be a memorial to the LORD, for an everlasting sign which will not be cut off.

Isaiah 55:11, 13, NASB

Adam and Eve were created for one supreme purpose—to have fellowship with God. Scripture gives a lovely picture of this by recording how God came into the Garden to have fellowship with Adam and Eve in the cool of the day, when a refreshing breeze sprang up in the evening.

God gave Adam a job: He was to be the keeper of the Garden. He was there to protect it, to watch over it. Adam failed to do so. The first failing of the human race was in a man. The first failure actually noted in Scripture was that of the woman, but the man was delinquent in his duty. He failed to be where he should have been.

You see, this is the problem of our contemporary culture: delinquent males. It is men who have abdicated from their responsibility. Almost inevitably women have moved in to fill up the vacuum left by men, but that is never God's plan. God has one plan and it works.

The Unique Role of Women

My wife, Ruth, spoke frequently on the topic of being a woman of God. I regularly stole the following line from her, and I know she always forgave me. Ruth said that in the whole record of Creation there was nothing that was not good until man discovered he had no mate. That was the first occasion when God said something was not good: It was not good for man that he should be alone. Everything God had created was good up to that point, so woman has a special place. Without woman, man is not what he should be.

Here is the story from Genesis 2:19–22:

> Out of the ground the LORD God formed every beast of the field and every bird of the air, and brought them to Adam to see what he would call them. And whatever Adam called each living creature, that was its name. So Adam gave names to all cattle, to the birds of the air, and to every beast of the field. But for Adam there was not found a helper comparable to him [or, to complete him]. And the LORD God caused a deep sleep to fall on Adam, and he slept; and He took one of his ribs, and closed up the flesh in its place. Then the rib which the LORD God had taken from man He made [Hebrew, *He built*] into a woman, and He brought her to the man.

How did God build a rib into a woman? No explanation is given. Scriptural truths are often explained, but on this point the Bible is silent. The Lord then brought the woman to the man: "And Adam said: 'This is now bone of my bones and flesh of my flesh; she shall be called Woman'" (verse 23). In Hebrew, *man* is *iysh* and *woman* is *ishshah*. There is a direct relationship between the two words. "'She was taken out of Man.' Therefore a man shall leave his father and mother and be joined to his wife, and they shall become one flesh" (verses 23–24).

Questioning God's Word

Now, let's focus on the temptation that confronted Eve. Again, we remember that it was Adam's fault that Eve was left without his protection. He had allowed the serpent to get into the Garden.

> Now the serpent was more cunning than any beast of the field which the LORD God had made. And he said to the woman, "Has God indeed said, 'You shall not eat of every tree of the garden'?"
>
> Genesis 3:1

Notice that the serpent did not immediately deny the word of God. He questioned it. When Eve entertained his question, she was defeated. Likewise, the moment we permit ourselves to question the Word of God, we are on the way to defeat.

If we look back at the history of the last hundred years or so, we see that toward the end of the nineteenth century a particular movement of theologians originated in Germany. These scholars debated the veracity of the Bible: Was it really the accurate inspired Word of God or simply a compilation of documents? That movement spread to other countries—to Norway, to Britain and finally to America. But the movement began in Germany and I do not think it coincidental—in

23

fact, I believe it was a direct result—that two German men subsequently came into power and caused more human suffering than almost any other individuals in human history. The first was Karl Marx and the second was Adolf Hitler. In my opinion, they were the direct products of a movement that questioned the validity of Scripture. When we entertain Satan's questions, we open the way for his power.

This was the position that Eve put herself into. So the serpent tightened his grip:

> "Has God indeed said, 'You shall not eat of every tree of the garden'?" And the woman said to the serpent, "We may eat the fruit of the trees of the garden [she did not want to acknowledge that there were any limits]; but of the fruit of the tree which is in the midst of the garden, God has said, 'You shall not eat it, nor shall you touch it, lest you die.'" Then the serpent said to the woman, "You will not surely die. For God knows that in the day you eat of it your eyes will be opened, and you will be like God, knowing good and evil."
>
> Genesis 3:1–5

We cannot afford to entertain Satan's questions about the Scriptures. To do so may sound like intellectual inquiry. It may even sound intellectually honest, but it is the way to disaster.

All of us are probably familiar with the tragic scene that followed. Eve ate of the Tree of the Knowledge of Good and Evil. Then she gave the fruit to her husband, and they both ate. As a result, their eyes were opened. When they got knowledge, do you know the first awareness they had? They knew they were naked. Soon after that, they were expelled from the Garden.

In Spite of It All

But that is not the end of the story. God in His infinite mercy did not give up on the human race. He had a plan and He was determined to fulfill it. We catch a glimpse of this from a verse in the book of James. There are as many different ways of interpreting this verse as there are translations, but I will give you what I believe to be the right way. It happens to come from the New American Standard Version—and it makes sense. James 4:5 says, "Do you think that the Scripture speaks to no purpose: 'He jealously desires the Spirit which He has made to dwell in us'?"

God jealously desires the Spirit that He has caused to dwell in us. When God breathed Himself into man, He established a love relationship that He has never been willing to cancel or revoke. In spite of all the evil that we have done, in spite of all the tragedies and disasters that sin has brought upon us, God jealously desires the Spirit that He caused to dwell in us.

Some people dislike the phrase that *God is a jealous God*. To me, it is an amazing example of God's condescension—that He is willing to be jealous for people like you and me. It says that God wants our love so much He is jealous if we love in a way that is contrary to Him. So we see that in due time over the centuries, God worked out a plan to reconcile man to Himself. And that plan was Jesus.

God's Redemptive Heart

One of my favorite stories in Scripture for showing this out-working of God's redemptive plan is the story of Zacchaeus. The story begins this way: "Jesus entered and passed through Jericho. Now behold, there was a man named Zacchaeus who was a chief tax collector, and he was rich" (Luke 19:1–2).

Not only was Zacchaeus rich, he was also hated. The Jewish people hated those (like Zacchaeus) who collected taxes from them on behalf of the Romans. Those people were usually dishonest, making illegitimate gains for themselves.

When Zacchaeus heard that Jesus was passing that way, he wanted to see Him "but could not because of the crowd, for he was of short stature. So he ran ahead and climbed up into a sycamore tree to see Him, for He was going to pass that way" (verses 3–4).

If you go on a tour in Israel, the guides will probably take you to *the* sycamore tree in Jericho. Now, of course, it is not *the* sycamore tree. But what they will point out to you (which is very interesting) is that a sycamore tree has smooth bark and its branches begin rather high up the trunk. So, in other words, to climb a sycamore tree is not easy. I do not know what Zacchaeus did to get up into the branches of that tree. Maybe he jumped up, caught hold of the lowest branch and pulled himself up. Regardless, it required a lot of effort on his part.

Furthermore, he put himself in a rather undignified position; a wealthy man would generally not climb trees! Nonetheless, that is what he did. He just wanted one glimpse of Jesus. He likely expected that, as Jesus passed by, he would be able to see Him above the heads of the crowd. Something happened, however, that Zacchaeus had never anticipated. When Jesus got to the place where Zacchaeus was perched above, He stopped. Jesus looked up and saw him and said, "Zacchaeus, make haste and come down, for today I must stay at your house" (verse 5).

I notice from Scripture that Jesus never had to be introduced to anybody. No one said to Him, "That's Zacchaeus the tax collector." Jesus knew him immediately. Zacchaeus may or may not have known how significant it was that Jesus said, "I want to stop at your house tonight," but he climbed down and walked immediately with Jesus to his house. Many of those around this unlikely pair were criticizing Jesus' decision: "He's gone to be a guest with the tax collector, a man who takes unfair taxes." But Zacchaeus was a changed man.

Then Zacchaeus stood and said to the Lord, "Look, Lord, I give half of my goods to the poor; and if I have taken anything from anyone by false accusation, I restore fourfold." And Jesus said to him, "Today salvation has come to this house."

Luke 19:8–9

Parenthetically, one thing I notice about salvation is that it affects what we do with our money. If someone claims to be saved and never changes the way he handles his money, I doubt that he is saved. Zacchaeus's eyes were open to God's redemptive plan, and he experienced salvation.

God Never Gave Up

This is just one example of the truth that God never gave up on that breath that He breathed into that body of clay. In fact, ultimately He sent Jesus to bring it back to Himself. As Jesus declared at the house of Zacchaeus, "The Son of Man has come to seek and to save that which was lost" (Luke 19:10, NASB). That is why Jesus came. He came for the descendants of Adam, who were cut off from the Father, lost in the sins of rebellion and pride. Without Him we would have no hope of reaching our destiny.

Jesus came to save us, the Adamic race, into which God had breathed His very life. That is how valuable we are in the sight of God.

3

Discover Yourself in God's Mirror

Blessed be God, who has not turned away my
prayer, nor His mercy from me!

Psalm 66:20

In a teaching I once gave titled "Who Am I?" I used the
subtitle "Discover Yourself in God's Mirror." That gives
a hint of where we need to go next to understand our
identity and how valuable we are. The aim of this chapter is
to hold up a particular mirror in which you can see yourself.
But you will not be seeing your outward visible form. You
will be looking upon something you cannot see in any other
mirror: You will see what you are really like inside.

Looking for the Answer

Before I get into this subject, I want to cover a little of my
personal background because it is relevant to this theme. From

29

the time I came to know the Lord Jesus Christ personally—and I met Him one midnight in a barrack room of the British army in July 1941—there have been two truths I have never doubted. First, Jesus is alive. Second, the Bible is true. I came to both those conclusions in one night—the night I was saved.

But let me tell you how I came to them. Before that night in the barrack room, I was a professional philosopher. I can imagine that you do not meet many professional philosophers. In fact, there are not many—which is probably a good thing! When I say that I was a professional philosopher, I mean that I earned my living by it. It was not a very substantial living, but it kept me alive.

I became a philosopher because I was looking passionately for an answer. I believe I was one of those people who are born with questions inside. My questions were: *What is the purpose of life? What are we here for? What is worth doing, and what is not worth doing?*

I grew up in the nominal church in Britain, but I did not think that I would find an answer there. So when I went to King's College in Cambridge at the age of eighteen, I decided that I would look for an answer in philosophy.

Philosophy means "the love of the search for wisdom." I have the kind of mind that is at home in the abstract and does not like to get bogged down in practical details. For example, there are only two things I know about a car. One is that it goes and the other is that it stops. My aim with cars has always been to know somebody who knows more about them than I do!

For seven years at Cambridge—as a student and then holding a fellowship at the college—I pursued extensively the study of philosophy, and I can say objectively that I was successful in my field.

But I did not find the answer I was looking for.

That Baffling Book

Then World War II came along and I was uprooted. (I realized afterward that this was actually a good thing.) When I was called up into the army, my big problem was what I would take with me to read. Certainly, in the army you cannot carry a library around with you. Besides, books are heavy and you have to carry them yourself. So I thought to myself, *There's one book that really is a book of philosophy and, actually, it's probably the most widely read book in the world. It may well be the most influential book in human history. And I know very little about what's in that book.*

The book I had in mind was the Bible. I decided that it was my philosophic duty to study it. I bought myself a nice new black Bible. (I could not conceive of ever having any other color but black.) I took that Bible with me into the army and started to read it.

Well, I started at the beginning and found it to be the first book that really baffled me. I could not make heads or tails of it. I could not even classify it, other than being boring. But I determined that no book was going to beat me and set my face to read it through to the end. After nine months of struggling with this book came the night I met the Author. And the next day the book made perfect sense. The change was not gradual. It was instantaneous from one day to the next.

From 1941 onward I have been studying the Bible. Each day I read the Word, and each day I find it richer, more exciting and more illuminating than the day before. The more I read it, the more I see there is to learn in it.

One final point about my background. God called me specifically, verbally, in 1944 when I was still in the British army in Palestine, to be a teacher of the Scriptures. It was as clear and precise as anything that has ever happened in my life. From that point on, I sought to do that. Over many years I had the privilege of traveling widely, ministering to Christians of many different national and denominational and cultural backgrounds.

The Need for a Solid Foundation

I tell this story to give you an idea of my search to understand the relevance of life, and the answer I found. Through the years I have had wide acquaintance with the Body of Christ. I love God's people, and I thank God for what He is doing through the earth. But I have one deep concern as a Bible teacher. It seems to me that the majority of God's people do not have a strong, solid foundation of biblical knowledge. They may go to conventions and conferences, or maybe even schools, where they get a lot of different pieces of information, but in many cases they do not have any structure to assemble them into.

In this regard, God gave me a mental picture of somebody who buys an empty lot in order to build a house. This person assembles all the materials needed for a house, but never lays the foundation. Or, if he does lay the foundation, he never raises the bearing wall. Consequently, there is really nothing he can do with all the materials he has gathered.

So that person goes to a convention, comes back and tells his friend, "Look at this wonderful marble bathtub I bought. Isn't it beautiful?" Well, it is a beautiful bathtub. But what do you do with a bathtub if you have no plumbing system? You can admire it, but it is difficult to make any use of it.

Then he goes to another convention and comes back and says, "Look at this beautiful oak front door I got." But he cannot do much with a door if he does not have a wall to place it in.

This brings us to the vast subject of the nature of man. It includes psychology, physiology and many other "ologies" that I am not competent to teach. What I can provide for you, however, is a framework into which you can fit the specific areas of knowledge you acquire.

Say, for instance, you are studying to be a counselor. In school and various internships you learn about psychology and other aspects of important truths. The problem is that it is dangerous to have these topics isolated on their own, away from the total context of biblical truth. It is very easy to go into error, to become one-sided and to become ineffective in really helping people. This is the case with any profession or vocation or church ministry. In the last resort, what all people need is the truth of God's Word. Nothing else is sufficient.

So my primary drive in every place and on every occasion has been to provide a foundation. Simple, practical, theologically uncomplicated. A foundation upon which people can then build all the wonderful truths that they subsequently glean or that they have already gleaned. That is why I produced a set of books known as the *Foundation Series* (now titled *Foundational Truths for Christian Living*). My aim was to present in a clear, simple way the great truths that are the basis of the Christian faith. And that is why the question "Who am I?"— my identity in the scheme of things—is so important.

Looking at a True Reflection

And that is the premise for seeing ourselves in a special mirror, for you have discerned by now that the mirror in which we see ourselves as we really are is God's Word.

First, let me justify the use of the word *mirror* by turning to the first chapter of the epistle of James. He is speaking about what you can expect the Word of God to do for you, and he says, in effect, it is like a mirror. But he goes on to say, "You had better make the right use of the mirror."

Here are his words:

> But be doers of the word, and not hearers only, deceiving yourselves. For if anyone is a hearer of the word and not a doer, he is like a man observing his natural face in a mirror; for he observes himself,

goes away, and immediately forgets what kind of man he was. But he who looks into the perfect law of liberty and continues in it, and is not a forgetful hearer but a doer of the work, this one will be blessed in what he does.

James 1:22–25

James raises this question: "What if you take an ordinary mirror, look into it, see what you look like, discover that your face is dirty, your clothes are stained, your hair is unkempt? What would be the use of then going away and forgetting what you saw in the mirror without doing anything about it?"

James applies this same logic in a spiritual sense. He says that when we look into the mirror of God's Word, we see something that is not revealed anywhere else: our inward nature. And when we see that in God's mirror, James says that we had better act on what we see. If our hair is untidy, we need to comb it. If our faces are dirty, we need to wash them. If our clothes are unclean or ragged, we need to have them cleaned or repaired. We must act upon what we see.

The Paradox of Mankind

In order to understand our true reflection, we need to examine some paradoxical aspects of mankind—notably, how such a humble being could fill a place of infinite magnitude in God's plans.

It is actually the psalmist David who raises the question of our value and identity in light of this paradox. He asks, "What is man that You should even consider him, Lord?" Let's turn to Psalm 8 and read the verses in which David ponders this.

When I consider Your heavens, the work of Your fingers, the moon and the stars, which You have ordained; what is man that You take thought of him, and the son of man that You care for him? Yet You have made him a little lower than God [*Elohim*, the usual word for

"God," can also be translated "angels"], and You crown him with glory and majesty! You make him to rule over the works of Your hands; You have put all things under his feet, all sheep and oxen, and also the beasts of the field, the birds of the heavens and the fish of the sea, whatever passes through the paths of the seas.

Psalm 8:3–8, NASB

In these verses we have two paradoxes showing that man— the creature of humble origin—has tremendous destiny and potential. First, man is just a little tiny speck in the immensity of God's universe. When we consider in the context of modern physics the immeasurable immensity of the universe, we have to echo David's question: What is man?

In addition the Bible says without apology that men are like grasshoppers on the face of the earth (see Isaiah 40:22). Even that gives us more status in proportion to the total dimensions of the universe than is accurate. Man is just a tiny speck in a vast universe that he can never fully explore and never fully control. And yet somehow, God is very concerned about him.

The second paradox found here is the fact that humankind has been made just a little lower than God. The purpose for this was to make him a ruler. Looking back in Genesis we read:

> Then God said, "Let us make man in our image, in our likeness, and let them rule over the fish of the sea and the birds of the air, over the livestock, over all the earth, and over all the creatures that move along the ground."
>
> Genesis 1:26, NIV

Everything in the earth was put under the feet of man and woman for them to rule. We find that drive still in mankind today—that innate sense that we ought to be ruling, that craving to rule. Yet the paradox is that we cannot rule ourselves. Because we yielded to temptation and missed our destiny, we are plagued with every kind of personal problem and weakness. We have so many problems in relationship to our fellow man that the earth is filled with war, hatred, violence and mistrust. Yet there is a sense in us that we are destined to rule.

Actually, we find a third paradox, which is shown in this verse above from Genesis. Notice again that God speaks in the plural: "Let *Us* make man in *Our* image, in *Our* likeness." God is one and yet more than one.

This idea of unity and plurality in the innermost nature of God Himself is defined in the opening verse of the Bible: "In the beginning God created." The Hebrew word for God is *Elohim*, which is plural in form, but the word for *created* in Hebrew is singular. So in the beginning, a plural God created in the singular. As the Bible progresses, it unfolds the three Persons who make up the one God: Father, Son and Holy Spirit. Triune: three and yet one.

Here we see the third paradox and mention again an exciting revelation that we will begin to explore in the next section: Man and woman, who are created in the likeness of God, are also triune beings—one personality yet three elements.

So we see the paradoxes of man. First, we are but tiny specks in the immensity of the universe, yet greatly cared for by God. Second, we see the conflict between our destiny to rule and our plaguing weaknesses. And, third, the human personality is a triune being created in the likeness of a triune God. It is this last paradox that will form the basis of our continuing study to understand why God gave us the inner nature He did, what happened to it at the Fall and how He offers to regenerate it.

Looking with X-ray Vision

First Thessalonians 5:23 gives us the Bible's picture, or revelation, of total human personality, the three parts of our nature. It is contained in a prayer of Paul for the believers he is writing to:

> Now may the God of peace Himself sanctify you entirely; and may your spirit and soul and body be preserved complete, without blame at the coming of our Lord Jesus Christ.
>
> NASB

Notice the words there *entirely* and *complete*. In describing the total human personality, Paul presents it in three elements. "May your spirit and soul and body be preserved complete." This is the Bible's revelation of the full inner nature of humankind: the spirit (which has direct contact with God), the soul (the decision maker) and the body (the outward visible nature).

Just as God's Word defines the elements of our total inner personality, so it shows us what we are really like inside. No other mirror will show us that. We could say, in a sense, that God's Word uses X-ray vision. It reveals what cannot be seen with ordinary eyes. This truth is stated in Hebrews:

> For the word of God is living and active. Sharper than any double-edged sword, it penetrates even to dividing soul and spirit, joints and marrow; it judges the thoughts and attitudes of the heart. Nothing in all creation is hidden from God's sight. Everything is uncovered and laid bare before the eyes of him to whom we must give account.
>
> Hebrews 4:12–13, NIV

God's X-ray mirror is like a surgeon's scalpel. It penetrates even to that innermost, invisible nature of every human, which is made up of soul and spirit.

In fact, without this mirror of God's Word, no one can really know how his own inner nature is constructed and interrelated. Nor, without the revelation of the Bible, can anyone fully understand the nature of soul and spirit and their relation to the body. Only the Bible can divide between these components that are so intimately connected and reveal what is there.

The next chapters of this book will delve into a full understanding of the three elements that make up human personality. Without question, the only accurate source of this understanding is the Bible. I have studied many, many human attempts to discern the real nature of man, to understand *who* we are and *why* we are. Trust me when I say that none of them provides a satisfying answer. Human wisdom only leaves us baffled. But when we look by faith in the mirror of God's Word, then and then alone do we understand our own inner being.

What is our value? Our true identity? In the course of this book I will do my best to hold up this mirror and invite you to look in it. I believe that it will become clearer and clearer to you why you matter so much to God.

4

Spirit, Soul and Body

Therefore the LORD longs to be gracious to you,
and therefore He waits on high to have compassion on you. For the LORD is a God of justice; how
blessed are all those who long for Him.

Isaiah 30:18, NASB

The human personality is a topic that is rarely dealt with. In this chapter we will explore the relationships among the three elements of mankind—the spirit, the soul and the body. As we understand the primary roles of each part of our triune being, God's plan for how they interact, and what the corresponding activities are in those roles, we learn how to operate effectively in each area. This will help us discern what godly activity the three elements should engage in and the ungodly activities that we should avoid.

I want to mention here that in chapters to come, we will study the devastating effects on each of the three elements as a result of our rebellion against God at the Fall—a catastrophic occurrence. We will then learn more about God's plan of regeneration for the spirit, soul and body, for He continued to love His creation. And we will also discover that even when we have been reborn into new life in Christ, we can still rebel and hinder the working of the spirit, soul and body that God intended. Finally, we will explore the thrilling changes that will occur in the total human personality when Christ comes for His people.

But that is all to come as we delve more deeply into the question of how much we matter to God. Let's begin here with the working together of the spirit, soul and body according to God's good plan.

Introduction to the Three Elements

Most people (except philosophers) have little problem with a person having a body. (I remember one entire semester spent discussing whether or not our bodies were really there!) Basically, though, we all agree that we have a body. I am sure, as well, that most Christians acknowledge that we have a soul. But many, many Christians are not aware that we also have a spirit and that the soul and spirit are distinct from one another. Anyone involved in any form of psychology would confirm that the majority of contemporary secular psychologists do not acknowledge the spirit as something distinct from the soul.

I once taught in a Bible college in western Canada where the name of every course had to end in *ology*. The study of the Church was *ecclesiology*; the study of salvation was *soteriology*; the study of the Holy Spirit was *pneumatology*. The subject I had to teach was theology, and it was rather dull.

Anyway, I had to teach from a particular textbook and, although it was a Pentecostal Bible college, the textbook was not prepared by a Pentecostal author. This textbook acknowledged only soul and body; it saw no difference between spirit and soul. I ran into continual problems teaching from that textbook. That experience made me very aware that we are obscuring an important truth if we fail to see the differences between spirit and soul.

Our modern languages tell us something interesting about the Greek words that are used in the New Testament for these three elements that make up the personality. The word for *spirit* in Greek is *pneuma,* which also means "wind" or "breath." Some English words derive from it, like *pneumatic,* indicating something that works by breath or wind. The word for *soul* in Greek is *psuche,* which gives us many English words such as *psychology.* The word for *body* in Greek is *soma.* A familiar use of the words for *soul* (*psuche*) and *body* (*soma*) is the English word *psychosomatic.* This word indicates that a particular problem should not be attributed to one's body alone or one's soul alone because it stems from both.

Interesting enough is the fact of the paucity of words in English (and other similar languages) that begin with *pneuma,* the word for *spirit.* What does this mean? It means simply that it is likely for someone to be aware he has a soul, but that it is very unlikely for him to be aware of his own spirit. His spirit is an element that goes deeper than his understanding. He cannot plumb it on his own; he can know about it only through divine revelation. So again we see that we are absolutely dependent upon the mirror of God's Word if we want to know the truth about ourselves.

The Chain of Command

In a nutshell, the spirit is God-conscious, the soul is self-conscious and the body is world-conscious. The distinctions between

41

them are important factors in how we behave. Whenever a person is wrapped up in himself or herself, for instance, you know that person is living in the realm of the soul. The realm of the spirit releases us from selfishness and self-centeredness.

Spirit: God-Conscious

The supreme function of the spirit is union and communion with God. The spirit should not be dictated to from below (one's soul and body); it should be directed from above (the Holy Spirit). God's Spirit came down into man's spirit. A human's spirit, therefore, is the highest of the three elements.

One of the most amazing statements in the Bible is found in 1 Corinthians 6. In this passage, Paul is warning against immorality. He begins by saying, "Do you not know that he who is joined to a harlot [a prostitute] is one body with her? For 'the two,' He says, 'shall become one flesh' " (verse 16). In that context, Paul goes on to say: "But he who is joined to the Lord is one spirit with Him" (verse 17).

I trust I will not offend you by observing a direct correspondence between sexual union in the flesh and spiritual union with God. That is how real it is. Just as surely as a man and woman can be united sexually, so one's spirit can be united with God spiritually.

Here is a very important example of where we must not confuse the spirit with the soul. Paul says that the one joined to the Lord is *one spirit* with Him. It would be completely incorrect to say that the union produces one soul. This is the great privilege given to the human spirit through Jesus' atoning sacrifice—to have direct, personal union with God.

The result of the human spirit's direct contact with God is a reproduction of God's attitudes and responses. Here are two examples—first from the life of Jesus, then from the life of Paul.

The gospels tell us these three things about Jesus' relation to the Holy Spirit: He sighed in Spirit, He rejoiced in Spirit and He groaned in Spirit. When Scripture says *in Spirit*, it is making a careful distinction from the soul. Jesus reproduced God's attitude and God's response in each of those three situations. His sigh was the sigh of God over a generation demanding a "sign" (see Mark 8:12). His rejoicing was over the people who had responded to the Gospel in a simple, childlike manner (see Luke 10:21). And His groaning was over the awful sadness of Lazarus's death (see John 11:33).

Scripture also speaks of the Spirit in the life of Paul in various passages. Paul "purposed in the Spirit, when he had passed through Macedonia and Achaia, to go to Jerusalem, saying, 'After I have been there, I must also see Rome'" (Acts 19:21). This means that God's purpose for Paul became so much part of his spirit, it became his own purpose as well.

Do you see the pertinence for us as followers of Jesus? We need to ask ourselves, *When I purpose things, do I purpose them in my spirit or in my flesh?* Paul is saying, in effect, "I am not changeable. When I get God's purpose, that settles it, because I purpose in the Spirit."

In the next chapter we read that Paul says,

> And see, *now I go bound in the spirit* to Jerusalem, not knowing the things that will happen to me there, except that the Holy Spirit testifies . . . that chains and tribulations await me. But none of these things move me; nor do I count my life dear to myself, so that I may finish my race with joy.
>
> Acts 20:22–24, emphasis added

Because he was purposed to God's will in his spirit, he was bound before he was ever imprisoned. In other words, God's destiny for him to be imprisoned was already so fixed in his spirit, he was affected by it before he was actually physically bound.

I believe that a lot of people serve God not in the spirit but in the soul, the function we observe next.

Soul: Self-Conscious

The soul, in a way, is wrapped up in itself. It was the philosopher Descartes who said, "I think, therefore I am." Typical of a philosopher, he had to prove to himself that he existed. But you see, what he was talking about was the realm of the soul. He knew his soul was real because he thought.

You might think of the soul as the ego. *Ego* is the Latin word for *I*. The soul makes the decisions. When you read about an evangelistic campaign giving the number of "decisions for Christ," do you know what made each decision? The soul. It is the soul that gets saved. The soul says, "I will receive Jesus," and salvation follows. If the soul says, "Don't give me that stuff!" then the soul is lost. Every human being without Christ is a lost rebel wandering aimlessly, not knowing the fact of his immense value to the Creator.

The soul is divided into three areas: the mind (or intellect), the will and the emotions. The *mind* says, "I think," "I reason," "I imagine" and a lot of other thought-related functions. The *will* says, "I want." That is one of the first phrases most children learn to say. The *emotions* say, "I feel."

An unregenerate person is controlled by those three phrases: *I think*, *I want* and *I feel*. That is what makes him act. Some people are more motivated by "I want," some people more by "I think" and some people more by "I feel," but that is the nature of the soul.

Matthew 16:24–25 reveals an important condition attached to the soul:

Jesus said to His disciples, "If anyone desires to come after Me, let him deny himself, and take up his cross, and follow Me. For whoever desires to save his life [soul] will lose it, but whoever loses his life [soul] for My sake will find it."

This text, by the way, is another case where the word translated "life" is really "soul," *psuche*.

These verses tell us that in order to follow Jesus, you have to do three things: You must deny yourself (your soul), take up your cross and then follow Him. If you do not deny yourself and if you do not take up your cross, you cannot follow Him. It is impossible. I do not know what will happen to you in eternity, but in this life you cannot follow Jesus unless you make those first two steps.

What does it mean to deny? It means to say no. So how do you deny your soul? You say no to your soul. In other words, your soul says, "I think." You respond, "What you think is not important. It's what God's Word says that matters." Your soul says, "I want." You say, "It's not what you want that matters. It's God's will that matters." Your soul says, "I feel." You say, "What you feel is not important. It is the impressions of the Holy Spirit that matter."

In order to follow Jesus we have to say no to "I think," no to "I want," and no to "I feel." Multitudes of people sincerely trying to follow Jesus cannot do it because they have never learned to say no to their souls. Their souls still dictate the way they live. You cannot live for Christ and live for your soul. This is, in a way, the most critical point in the life of the Christian. But Jesus says that when you lose your soul then you find something of infinitely more value.

Body: World-Conscious

Now we come to the body, which is world-conscious through the five senses. Here is an important factor: In this present age in which we live, the spirit cannot give direction to the body. The spirit can make suggestions to the soul, but the soul makes all the decisions, communicates them to the body and the body acts them out.

A direct example of this interactive relationship appears in Psalm 103:1–2, a well-known psalm of David. He says, "Bless the LORD, O my soul; and all that is within me, bless His holy name!" Can you guess in this case what is talking to David's soul? It is his spirit. You see, through faith and repentance David's spirit had come back into contact with God. His natural spirit was restored. It was not re-created, for re-creation of the spirit could not happen until after the death and resurrection of Jesus Christ. That is New Testament salvation, the new birth. The Old Testament saints and prophets, through faith, came back into a relationship in which their original spirits were revived and came into living contact with God.

Here in Psalm 103 David wants to praise the Lord. Actually, it is his spirit that wants to praise the Lord, but his spirit cannot get it to happen. The spirit has to work through the soul. So the spirit says, "Come on, soul, wake up! Don't be so dull and sluggish. It's time to praise the Lord." His soul agrees and, in turn, motivates or activates the body. Then out of David's mouth come the words of praise.

Another example of the body acting out the direction of the soul and spirit is found in Hebrews 10:5 (quoting Psalm 40, which is a prediction of the Messiah): "Sacrifice and offering You did not desire, but a body You have prepared for Me." Why did God prepare a body for the Messiah? Verse 7 explains: "Then I said, 'Behold, I have come—in the volume of the book it is written of Me—to do Your will, O God.'" The Messiah received a body to do the will of God, as directed by His soul and spirit.

The fact that the spirit cannot operate the body directly is a kind of limitation for the spirit. I know of only one exception: speaking in tongues. Granted, this experience is not independent of the soul, because the soul has to say, "Okay, go ahead," and if the soul says, "No, I won't do it," it won't happen. But once the soul says, "Okay, go ahead," the soul sits back and the spirit controls the tongue. And the tongue does exactly what the spirit wants it to do.

Let me just mention that while you are speaking in tongues you will never say one wrong word. Never. You will never say anything that does not glorify God. "Your tongue," David says, "is your glory" (see Psalm 16:9; see also Acts 2:26). It is given to you for the supreme purpose of glorifying God. When the Holy Spirit controls your spirit, and your spirit controls your tongue, your tongue all that time will do what it was created to do.

I believe that is why the experience of speaking in tongues is so tremendously significant. As far as I can think, it is the only situation in this present age in which your spirit directly operates your body. Certainly, there may be other specific supernatural experiences that people have, but this is one that is open to every Christian.

I remember the first time I had the experience of speaking in tongues. I had been searching, searching, searching for something that would satisfy. I tried the highbrow—the ballet, the opera, travel. I tried the lowbrow—and I won't tell you how low my brow went. I tried everything. The more I tried, the thirstier I got. I did not even know what I was thirsty for, but the moment the Holy Spirit came in, I said, "This is it!" You know what I said next? I wanted to know why no one had ever told me about this in the church for all the years that I went there.

I praise God for speaking in tongues. My first wife, Lydia, who is with the Lord now, was a real warrior of the Lord. She came into the baptism in the Holy Spirit in Denmark when it was very unfashionable. In fact, she was a teacher in the

Danish state school, and her experience was so extraordinary that her case went up to the Danish Parliament to determine whether a teacher who spoke in tongues could remain in the state school. Incidentally, the answer was yes, thank God. Lydia resigned, however, and went to Jerusalem instead of remaining in the Danish school system.

The reason why I cite Lydia's experience is this: Hardly a day in her life passed (and she lived a long life) without her saying, "Thank You, God, for speaking in tongues." She enjoyed it to the last day of her life. She thought it was perhaps the highest privilege of her Christian experience. I would advise you never to belittle speaking in tongues. Never regard it as commonplace. It is unique.

A Typical Example of the Interrelationship

To give you a clearer picture of the proper interrelationship of these three elements, spirit, soul and body, I want to focus on one particular type of experience as an example. This example shows us how each element of the human personality has corresponding expressions—in the spirit, in the soul and in the body. In giving this example, I am, as you will see, choosing to use certain words in a rather specific way.

In the area of the body, let's take the experience of physical pleasure or pain. In the area of the soul, the related experience is happiness or unhappiness. And in the area of the spirit, the related experience is joy.

This helps us distinguish between what we have in the soul and what we have in the spirit. You see, happiness depends on circumstances; therefore, it is changeable. But joy depends on God alone; therefore, it is unchangeable. We can be very unhappy and yet have joy. It is the same with the body. We might experience good or ill, but that does not change the fact of joy in our spirits.

I always picture these particular expressions of the three elements of human personality in situations like this one: A young man in his sports car on a spring day with his girlfriend beside him is driving down the road. The sun is warm on his face; the wind is blowing his hair. He feels as though he owns the world. He is happy. Six months later, it is winter and his girlfriend has jilted him. His car is broken down, and it is raining. He is soggy and unhappy.

That describes happiness. It depends on situations and circumstances—your health, your financial state, the way your husband or your wife is treating you. Because of those circumstances, happiness fluctuates. Not that there is anything wrong with happiness. I like happiness. But we cannot expect to have happiness all the time.

Joy is different. Joy is a thing of the spirit and depends only on God. In Psalm 43:4, David says, "Then will I go to the altar of God, to God, my joy and my delight. I will praise you with the harp, O God, my God" (NIV). In the context of this psalm, David is downcast. He is depressed. Things are going against him. He is unhappy. But he recognizes the solution for unhappiness. It is to get back in touch with God through his spirit. God does not change. There are no circumstances with God. He is the great invariable, unchanging, eternal source of joy.

In the New Testament, Paul confirms this: "Not only is this so, but we also rejoice in God through our Lord Jesus Christ, through whom we have now received reconciliation" (Romans 5:11, NIV).

Incidentally, I believe in a sense that rejoicing in God is the ultimate of Christian experience. It is the spirit related to God, ruling the whole being. Though circumstances may be against us, joy is still ours in the Spirit through an unchanging relationship with an unchanging God. We need never be without joy.

What does this all mean? I believe it means that there must be divine order in each area of man's personality. First, the spirit must be in continuing union with God through the Holy Spirit.

Second, the soul must be in continuing submission to the spirit, in continuing self-denial. You remember that Jesus said, "You have to deny yourself daily." Every day the soul has to say, "No, I will not assert myself. I will yield to the Spirit."

And third, the body is set apart as God's temple and its members as yielded instruments for the service of the Holy Spirit. We will talk more about the body as God's temple in several chapters to come.

Giving and Receiving

Here, then, is the complete picture as God intended it. The Spirit, the eternal divine breath of God, breathed into a body of clay. The result was a living soul, something created and dependent on God not only to receive life but to maintain life.

This concept is beautifully conveyed by Paul: " 'Who has ever given to God, that God should repay him?' For from him and through him and to him are all things" (Romans 11:35–36, NIV). Everything comes from God. Everything is maintained by God. Everything returns to God.

This was God's plan, and it was perfect. But because of our steadfast determination to turn from the One who created and sustains and loves us, mankind has endured no end of trouble. In the next chapter, we will learn about the radical changes in the tripartite human personality caused by our rebellion.

5

Radical Rebellion

As for me, I said in my alarm, "I am cut off from
before Your eyes."

Psalm 31:22, NASB

Mankind has one basic problem: We are self-willed. In the words of the prophet Isaiah, "We all, like sheep, have gone astray, each of us has turned to his own way; and the LORD has laid on him [this is a prophetic picture of Jesus] the iniquity [or rebellion] of us all" (Isaiah 53:6, NIV).

All human problems ultimately go back to one root cause: rebellion against God. The very word *self-will* indicates the area in which this problem originates: the soul. The soul, the self, the ego, is, as we have learned, the decision-making function of the human personality. This tells us that self-will, or rebellion, originates in the soul—not in the spirit and not in the body.

Now that we understand God's intended functions for the three elements, let's look again at the tragic story of the Fall as recorded in Genesis 3. We will discover the outcome on the spirit, soul and body from our rebellion in the Fall and learn why we are so susceptible to temptation.

The Fall Times Three

First of all, beware if the devil asks you a question.

"Now the serpent was more cunning than any beast of the field which the LORD God had made. And he said to the woman, 'Has God indeed said, "You shall not eat of every tree of the garden"?' " (Genesis 3:1).

If you look at Genesis 2:16–18 you will notice that God gave His instructions about the trees to the man, not to the woman. Who told the woman? The man did. It was his job. God had said to Adam, "The day that you eat of it you shall surely die."

The woman was unwise, because she should not have answered the serpent. A friend of mine, who is a preacher, says that at that point Eve should have said, "I never talk to strange snakes without my husband!" How different history would have been if she had refused to enter into dialogue! But she did not refuse. Let's read again the words of Genesis 3:2–4:

> The woman said to the serpent, "We may eat the fruit of the trees of the garden; but of the fruit of the tree which is in the midst of the garden, God has said, 'You shall not eat it, nor shall you touch it, lest you die.' " Then the serpent said to the woman, "You will not surely die."

Notice Satan's tactic. It has never changed. And why should he change it? It works. The one thing Satan attempts to do is break down our faith in the Word of God. He does not make a direct attack. He starts with a question. When we are silly enough to answer his question, then he presses in with three objectives.

First of all, he causes us to *doubt*; secondly, to *disbelieve*; and thirdly, to *disobey*. Let me say that if you disbelieve and do not repent, you *will* disobey. It is absolutely sure. Every time Satan comes, his tactics are the same. And through those three steps, he has undermined countless millions of lives.

The devil responded to Eve's answer with these words: " 'You will not surely die. For God knows that in the day you eat of it your eyes will be opened, and you will be like God, knowing good and evil.' So when the woman saw . . ." (verses 4–6).

It is important to see the descent in that word *saw*. Eve moved from the faith realm to the sense realm. She trusted her senses more than the word of God.

> So when the woman saw that the tree was good for food, that it was pleasant to the eyes, and a tree desirable to make one wise, she took of its fruit and ate. She also gave to her husband with her, and he ate.
>
> Genesis 3:6

We can compare Eve's actions to the three basic forms of temptation that John speaks about in his first epistle (see 1 John 2:16): the lust of the flesh ("It is good for food"), the lust of the eyes ("It is pleasant to look at"), and the pride of life ("It will make me wise"). *I am going to be clever*, she thought. *I will be as clever as God.*

Let me point out that the motivation here, in itself, was not evil. It is good to want to be like God. It is good to want to know good and evil. What then was the evil? This is very important. *The evil was the desire to be independent of God.*

53

In other words, the essence of sin is not the desire to do evil. Rather, it is the desire to be independent of God.

No one and no entity in the universe will ultimately be independent of God. God will not tolerate it. He gives a period of grace, but a day is coming when anything that is not submitted to God will be banished from heaven and earth, consigned to the place Jesus called "outer darkness."

It is not enough simply to stop doing bad things, for that does not necessarily mean the problem has been resolved. There is something in every fallen child of Adam that does not want to depend on God. I know I am not the only one who has that problem. Whenever I am confronted with a problem, even after nearly fifty years as a Christian, my instinctive reaction is, "What am I going to do about it?" Thank God I have come to the place where I am sensible enough to stop and say, "God, what should I do?"

But Adam and his descendants have a certain trait. The key word, if you can accept it, is that you and I are rebels. Paul calls this trait "the old man" (Ephesians 4:22). Interestingly enough, when Paul talks about the old man, he never talks about the old Jewish man or the old Gentile man or the old any-other-kind of man. There are later accretions of nationality and culture, but the basic rebel is the same in all of us.

The Spirit: Cut Off from God

As I understand it, in the Fall the spirit died. The spirit, which was intended to be God's inner ruler over the lower elements of soul and body, was cut off from God, the only source of life.

Scripture tells us Adam lived more than nine hundred years physically, but he died spiritually the moment he disobeyed. After that he was like an electrical apparatus that has become unplugged and is running on battery power. It will go on functioning, but it is running down all the time.

As Paul explains: "But because of his great love for us, God, who is rich in mercy, made us alive with Christ even when we were dead in transgressions—it is by grace you have been saved" (Ephesians 2:4–5, NIV). His point is that we were not dead physically but dead spiritually. He makes the same point again in vivid language in Ephesians 4:18, talking about the unbelieving Gentiles: "They [the Gentiles] are darkened in their understanding and separated from the life of God because of the ignorance that is in them due to the hardening of their hearts" (NIV).

Four words in this verse describe the condition of man in his rebellion: *darkened, separated, ignorant* and *hardened*. With the spirit cut off, we are spiritually dead, dead in trespasses and sins, dead as the result of disobedience or rebellion.

The Soul: The Point of Attack

We have observed from the Genesis account of the Fall that when our enemy comes along in the form of a serpent, he does not attack the spirit with his temptations—he attacks the soul. In my judgment, every major struggle and problem in the Christian life is fought out on the battlefield of the soul. Now we do not need to feel condemned by this. Every saint of God has gone through similar battles. That is just the result of the Fall. The important thing is to learn the devil's tricks and how to deal with them.

If the soul responds to temptation, something negative happens and Satan has succeeded in cutting off our direct contact with God. That is the essence of the result of the Fall. Paul follows this train of thought, making reference to trespasses and sins "in which you once walked according to the course of this world, according to the prince of the power of the air, the spirit who now works in the sons of disobedience" (Ephesians 2:2). Who is the spirit that works in the sons of disobedience? Satan. And do you see how he is working? As a spirit in the area of the soul.

The passage continues: "Among whom also we all once conducted ourselves" (verse 3). There is no exception. We were all in the same boat "fulfilling the desires of the flesh and of the mind, and were by nature children of wrath, just as the others." Why were we children of wrath? Because we were sons of disobedience.

In the Fall man's soul became infected with rebellion. The result of this infection in every succeeding generation is that we no longer need to be tempted from the outside. We have an inner force of rebellion latent in our souls.

Looking again at this verse we see Paul's further explanation: "Among them we too all formerly lived in the lusts of our flesh, indulging the desires of the flesh and of the mind, and were by nature children of wrath, even as the rest" (Ephesians 2:3, NASB). The word *lusts* there indicates rebellious or perverted desires. Once mankind had turned against God in rebellion, the potential for lust—perverted evil desire—resided in his soul. Temptation could come from within: "Each one is tempted when he is carried away and enticed by his own lust" (James 1:14, NASB).

The Body: Falling into Corruption

Through the Fall the body experienced corruption. Paul talks of it this way: "The sting of death is sin" (1 Corinthians 15:56). The poison of death was injected into man's body by his sin.

In Ephesians 4:22, we read that our conduct "grows [or is growing] corrupt according to the deceitful lusts." The key word to describe the physical nature of fallen man is *corrupt*. He is subject to corruption, decay, sickness and ultimately (and inevitably) physical death. The Greek version of "the deceitful lusts" actually says "the lusts of defeat." Satan was able to procure our downfall, our defeat, by deceiving us.

The Spread of Corruption

What was the effect of rebellion on the whole personality? I would sum it up this way: God had appointed the spirit to rule the soul and the soul to rule the body. But, responding to the temptation of Satan, the soul and the body united against the rule of the spirit and, as it were, dethroned the spirit from its God-appointed place of rulership in the human personality.

This rebellious combination of the soul and the body is described in the Bible by a variety of phrases including, in the New Testament, the *flesh*, the *body*, the *body of sin*. When we read those phrases, we need to understand that they do not refer merely to the physical body. They refer to that combination of soul and body united in rebellion against God. The *flesh*, then, means the fallen nature that mankind has inherited in the physical body through birth.

The distinctive word that describes the flesh, or the fallen nature, is, again, the word *corrupt*. Inwardly, mankind is morally corrupt. Outwardly, mankind is physically corrupt. And the nature of corruption is such that it is progressive. As the years pass, the evidence of corruption is more plainly seen in every area of the soul and body. Unless the process is arrested, we suffer the ongoing deterioration of human personality.

6

The Remedy Revealed

> Wondrously show Your lovingkindness, O
> Savior.
>
> Psalm 17:7, NASB

Thankfully, we do not have to stay in this deteriorated condition. Because God cares so much for you and for me, He wrought a miracle by which man's spirit can be brought back from death to life with Him.

First Corinthians 15, the great resurrection chapter, gives us this wonderful revelation:

> And so it is written, "The first man Adam became a living being [soul]." The last Adam became a life-giving spirit. . . . The first man was of the earth, made of dust; the second Man is the Lord from heaven.
>
> verses 45, 47

The name *Adam* in Hebrew is directly connected with the word for "earth," which is *adamah*. His name indicates that he was taken from the earth. This "first man," Adam, who was of the earth, became a living soul.

Another "Adam" is named here and this speaks of the Person who came in the fullness of God's time to save us: Jesus of Nazareth, the Lord from heaven.

Two different titles of Jesus are given in this verse, and it is very important to get them right. A lot of people get them wrong. First of all, He is called the "last Adam." Not the *second* Adam, but the *last* Adam. He was not last in the sense of historical sequence, but He was last in the sense that He was the end of the whole evil Adamic inheritance. When Jesus hung on the cross, He bore the total penalty for every transgression and disobedience, every sin and rebellion. When He died, that evil inheritance died. When He was buried, it was buried—closed off and shut away. He put away sin by the sacrifice of Himself and died as the last Adam.

When He rose from the dead three days later, He was "the second man," a new kind of man, the head of a totally new race that had never existed before. It is the God-man race—a race in which God and man are united in one nature. We could call it the Emmanuel race.

Through the resurrection of Jesus Christ, we are begotten again, or born again, out of sin and out of death into the new race of which Jesus is the head. Colossians 1:18 says that He is the head and we are the body. We know that the head comes first in a birth and the body follows. Jesus as the head has been born again from the dead, and we are part of His body. We are part of this new race through faith in His death and resurrection.

That is what we are born into through faith. If we believe in Jesus' atoning death and His triumphant resurrection, we become a new kind of being—one in which God and man are united in one person. That is our destiny as Christians.

Peter spoke of this in addressing believers: "Blessed be the God and Father of our Lord Jesus Christ, who according to His abundant mercy *has begotten us again* to a living hope through the resurrection of Jesus Christ from the dead" (1 Peter 1:3, emphasis added). Every person on earth has the opportunity to be part of this new creation.

On Resurrection Sunday evening, the risen Jesus appeared to His terrified disciples, shut away in a room. Jesus breathed upon them and said, "Receive holy breath," or "Receive the Holy Spirit." In a certain sense, at that moment the original creation was reenacted in a new creation. The same Person who had breathed the Spirit of life into the body of clay in the Garden breathed into those disciples a totally new kind of life. It was a life that had triumphed over sin, over death, over hell, over the grave and over Satan. They were born again. They came into New Testament salvation.

Everybody who becomes a true believer in Jesus Christ has an experience that corresponds to that one. You do not become a Christian by joining a church or even by being christened or baptized. The only way you can become a Christian is by meeting Jesus personally.

Jesus said, "I am the door. If anyone enters by Me, he will be saved" (John 10:9). You meet Him not in a physical presence but through the Holy Spirit, and He breathes into you exactly the same kind of life He breathed into the disciples in that Upper Room. By that action you are born again. Your spirit is brought back from death to life.

The Miracle of Rebirth

Rebellion left us defeated, miserable, insecure. But because God loves us so much, we can be possessors of life that is divine, eternal, incorruptible, undefeatable and indestructible. That is the kind of life you have inside you if you are His child. Can you see why you matter so much to God?

Jesus Himself was the first one to speak about this miracle of rebirth, or regeneration, in plain terms. He said that we cannot ever recover from the effects of our rebellion in any other way except through rebirth or regeneration.

This point is brought out clearly in the conversation He had with Nicodemus, the Pharisee:

> Jesus answered and said to him [Nicodemus], "Truly, truly, I say to you, unless one is born again [or reborn] he cannot see the kingdom of God." Nicodemus said to Him, "How can a man be born when he is old? He cannot enter a second time into his mother's womb and be born, can he?" Jesus answered, "Truly, truly, I say to you, unless one is born of water and the Spirit he cannot enter into the kingdom of God. That which is born of the flesh is flesh, and that which is born of the Spirit is spirit. Do not be amazed that I said to you, 'You must be born again [or you must be reborn].'"
>
> John 3:3–7, NASB

You see, Jesus emphasized that this experience is absolutely essential. There is no substitute. There is no alternative.

It is clear that Nicodemus was a good man and a religious man. But he did not understand what Jesus was talking about. He thought perhaps Jesus was talking about a second physical birth. The answer of Jesus indicates that He was referring not to a physical birth, but to a spiritual rebirth. Being born of the Spirit of God. Being reborn. This is the experience by which life from God is restored to man's dead spirit.

We could compare these statements to the words of Paul in his letter to the Ephesians:

> But God, being rich in mercy, because of His great love with which He loved us, even when we were dead in our transgressions [notice

that we were spiritually dead], made us alive together with Christ [made us again spiritually alive with Christ] (by grace you have been saved).

Ephesians 2:4–5, NASB

It is imperative that we understand that no system of law, no religion, however good, however sound, can give spiritual life to a person who is dead spiritually in transgression.

Paul brings this truth out clearly: "For if a law had been given that could impart life, then righteousness would certainly have come by the law" (Galatians 3:21, NIV). You see, a dead person needs one thing above all else: He needs life. Not rules; not religion; but spiritual life. The Bible reveals that this is received only by faith.

How the Seed Grows

How does regeneration take place? What is the process? I want to outline it for you very simply.

First of all, the new life comes out of a seed. The seed is the Word of God. Scripture says, "For you have been born again [reborn], not of perishable seed, but of imperishable, through the living and enduring word of God" (1 Peter 1:23, NIV). Jesus also made it clear: "The seed is the word of God" (Luke 8:11).

The Word of God received by faith into our hearts is like a seed, a seed that contains in it potentially the life of God. As is the nature of the seed, so is the nature of the life that comes out of the seed. Because the seed is divine, the life is divine. Because the seed is eternal, the life is eternal. Because the seed is incorruptible, or imperishable, so is the nature of the life that comes out of it. But it takes the supernatural operation of the Holy Spirit to cause that seed to germinate, to bring out the life that is latent within.

63

And so Jesus says, "That which is born of the Spirit [capital S for the Holy Spirit] is spirit" (John 3:6, NASB).

Once this seed is caused to germinate and the life comes out of it, that life reproduces the nature of Jesus Himself. Jesus, the personal Word, is produced out of the preached Word when it is made alive and caused to germinate by the Holy Spirit. It is very, very important to see that the new life, the new nature, the new spiritual being that comes out of the rebirth is the very nature of Jesus Himself, the personal Word of God received through the preached Word of God.

Paul says this:

> You are not in the flesh [you are not under the control of the old rebellious nature] but in the Spirit, if indeed the Spirit of God dwells in you. But if anyone does not have the Spirit of Christ, he does not belong to Him.
>
> Romans 8:9, NASB

You see, that which is produced in us by regeneration is the Spirit of Christ. And without the Spirit of Christ, we do not belong to Him. We may be religious, but we do not have life. Then Paul goes on to say: "If Christ is in you, though the body is dead because of sin, yet the spirit is alive because of righteousness" (verse 10, NASB).

The body is still under sentence of death—that is the ultimate end of the physical body until the resurrection. But within that body, the spirit is brought to life because of the righteousness of Jesus Christ imparted to us by faith.

So we see that out of the preached Word, the Holy Spirit brings forth by a miracle, a new life. This new life is the life of the personal Word—the life of Jesus Himself.

I believe that many people who are truly born again do not fully appreciate what God has placed inside them. One reason is that they do not look long enough in the mirror of God's Word to see what this new inner nature or personality is like.

The miracle of God's Word is that when we look, it first of all shows us our own lost and sinful and corrupt condition. But then if we accept God's remedy and begin to look again, it shows us the nature of the new personality that God has brought to birth within us.

Which Nature Shall We Choose?

Speaking about those who are born of God—reborn, regenerated—John makes this strong statement: "No one who is born of God practices sin, because His seed abides in him; and he cannot sin, because he is born of God" (1 John 3.9, NASB).

Let me state immediately here that I do not believe this statement means a born-again believer cannot sin. The way I understand what John says is that within the born-again believer, a new nature is born, a new life, that is absolutely incorruptible. The seed is incorruptible. The life is incorruptible. And that new nature is incapable of sinning. No one who is born of God practices sin. Why? Because God's seed—the incorruptible seed—abides in Him. Never can the life from that seed become corrupted. It is incorruptible.

John says further: "By this the children of God and the children of the devil are obvious: anyone who does not practice righteousness is not of God, nor the one who does not love his brother" (1 John 3:10, NASB). There are two kinds of children, two kinds of descendants. The children who are descended from God and the children who are descended from the devil. John says their conduct makes obvious whose children they are.

Bear that in mind. If you are born again, there is a life in you that cannot be defeated. In fact, that life will defeat the world. John also says, "For whatever is born of God overcomes the world; and this is the victory that has overcome

65

the world—our faith" (1 John 5:4, NASB). Whoever is born of God is born to overcome.

But this only becomes effective as we live it out in faith. "This is the victory that has overcome the world—our faith." In the new birth is the potential for victory. But in our faith is the actual realization of that victory.

Another attribute of this new life that is born in us is that it cannot be touched by the devil. The Bible says, "We know that no one who is born of God sins; but He who was born of God keeps him, and the evil one does not touch him" (1 John 5:18, NASB).

We are kept by Jesus, the firstborn of the dead, the eldest brother (see Romans 8:29). The evil one, Satan, cannot touch that new, regenerated nature. It is outside the territory that he can reach. He can touch a person's soul. He can touch a person's body. But he cannot touch the regenerated spirit. It is an undefeatable life, an undefeatable nature.

We also need to see that God has made full provision for every need of this new life:

> His divine power has given us everything we need for life and godliness through our knowledge of him who called us by his own glory and goodness. Through these he has given us his very great and precious promises, so that through them you may participate in the divine nature and escape the corruption in the world caused by evil desires [or lusts].
>
> 2 Peter 1:3–4, NIV

So you see, not only is the new life born of the incorruptible seed of the Word of God, but, even more, it feeds on the incorruptible Word of God. As it feeds on that Word, it becomes more and more a partaker of the divine nature. In proportion as it partakes of the divine nature, it is delivered from the corruption that is in this world through lust.

Thus, we have two natures in absolute opposition to one another. The old carnal nature, the flesh, is corruptible. The divine nature born in us is incorruptible. And neither nature can be changed. God's nature can never become corruptible, and the old nature can never become incorruptible. The way we live will be determined by which nature controls us.

The Unbroken Chain

Paul helps us understand the appropriation of this new nature in his letter to the Galatians: "I have been crucified with Christ and I no longer live, but Christ lives in me. The life I live in the body, I live by faith in the Son of God, who loved me and gave himself for me" (Galatians 2:20, NIV).

Paul is saying: "When I turned to Jesus Christ, and surrendered my life to Him, my old life died. That old life was dealt with by the death of Jesus on the cross. But a new life came up within me, and that is Christ living in me."

Notice again that Paul always emphasizes the need for faith. Great potential is available in the new birth, but the realization of that potential depends on the continuous exercise of active faith: "Christ lives in me. The life I live in this body I live by faith in the Son of God." In this way, God's purpose is fulfilled—that Jesus became the firstborn among many brothers. Through our regeneration we become sons of God and younger brothers of Jesus Christ.

This resembles a kind of unbroken chain. The Father sent Jesus, and Jesus depended on the Father for His ongoing life. But Jesus says, "The one who believes in Me is going to depend on Me for his or her ongoing spiritual life, just as I depend on the Father."

In the next two chapters, our focus will be an explanation of how spirit, soul and body function together after regeneration—if the chain remains unbroken. In chapter 9 we will explore what happens to someone whose soul turns back.

7

How It All Comes Together

"The LORD GOD is my strength and song, and
He has become my salvation." Therefore you
will joyously draw water from the springs of
salvation.

Isaiah 12:2–3, NASB

The highest element of mankind is the spirit. The essential result of regeneration is that your spirit is reunited with God and thus made alive again. It becomes able to receive the spiritual life of which God is the only source.

As we noted earlier, Paul describes this union of our spirits with God, through faith: "But the one who joins himself to the Lord is one spirit with Him" (1 Corinthians 6:17, NASB). Again, this is one of those occasions when it is important to understand the distinction between the spirit and the soul.

69

The spirit, not the soul, was created for union with God and cannot live out of union with God.

Let's look at the purpose of the spirit, soul and body as products of regeneration.

God's Purpose for the Spirit

In Bible times, the fuel for every lamp was olive oil. We might think of the rekindled spirit as such a lamp. The Holy Spirit then comes like oil to burn brightly and illuminate the inward nature, which was dark and alienated from God up to that time. In Proverbs 20:27 the writer says this: "The spirit of man is the lamp of the LORD, searching all the innermost parts of his being" (NASB).

Furthermore, the reborn spirit becomes a channel through which the Holy Spirit can flow out into this world. Jesus said,

> "He who believes in Me, as the Scripture said, 'From his innermost being will flow rivers of living water.'" But this He spoke of the [Holy] Spirit, whom those who believed in Him were to receive; for the Spirit was not yet given, because Jesus was not yet glorified.
>
> John 7:38–39, NASB

After the Holy Spirit was given on the Day of Pentecost, the regenerated human spirit became a channel—a riverbed—through which rivers of spiritual life can flow. That is a marvelous transformation because just before that, Jesus had said, "If anyone is thirsty, let him come to Me and drink."

Through this transformation, anyone who is thirsty and does not have enough for himself becomes a channel through which waters of spiritual life can flow out to the needy world around.

Worship, the First Function of the Spirit

I want to highlight three distinctive functions of the regenerated spirit; there are more, of course. The first is worship. In John 4:23–24, Jesus says this:

> But an hour is coming, and now is, when the true worshipers will worship the Father in spirit and truth; for such people the Father seeks to be His worshipers. God is spirit, and those who worship Him must worship in spirit and truth.
>
> NASB

Worship is a function of the regenerated spirit. It is the response of the spirit to the immediate presence of God, and God is looking for those who will worship Him in spirit and in truth.

Until our spirits are regenerated, we really do not know what worship is. It is the most intimate, the most beautiful, the most reverent attitude and relationship possible toward the living God. It is our response to the privilege of being united to God and knowing Him.

Fellowship, the Second Function of the Spirit

The second function of the regenerated spirit is fellowship—sharing with God, particularly sharing God's secrets. This is so precious to me. One of the ways in which the regenerated believer, filled with the Holy Spirit, is permitted to share God's secrets is through worshiping in an unknown language that the Spirit gives. This first happened on the Day of Pentecost and continued on through the New Testament record. I mentioned earlier that this is the only circumstance in which the spirit of man can bypass the soul (though needing the soul's agreement) and direct the body.

71

Paul makes certain statements about the function of the spirit when it is communicating with God in an unknown tongue. He says, "For one who speaks in a tongue [that is, an unknown tongue] does not speak to men but to God; for no one understands, but in his spirit he speaks mysteries" (1 Corinthians 14:2, NASB).

What a beautiful concept! The mind is inactive, but the spirit in this blessed communion with God is sharing God's secrets.

It is a beautiful fact of psychology that a person never shares his secrets with his enemies, but only with his closest friends. And so, when we are permitted to share God's secrets through this method of communion with God—in an unknown tongue—we are enjoying the fullest expression of friendship with God.

A little further on, in verse 14, Paul speaks about this again for he says, "For if I pray in a tongue, my spirit prays, but my mind is unfruitful" (NASB).

Once again, it is important to distinguish between the spirit and the soul. The mind is a function of the soul. There are times when the mind, as it were, is in neutral, but the spirit is in direct living communion with God. That happens as the spirit prays and the mind is left inactive. Of course, that is not the way we always pray. Many times we pray with our minds, too.

Revelation, the Third Function of the Spirit

The third distinctive function of the regenerated spirit is to receive revelation from God. Again we turn to the words of Paul:

However, as it is written: "No eye has seen, no ear has heard, no mind has conceived what God has prepared for those who love him"—but God has revealed it to us by his Spirit. The Spirit [of

God] searches all things, even the deep things of God. For who among men knows the thoughts of a man except the man's spirit within him? In the same way no one knows the thoughts of God except the Spirit of God. We have not received the spirit of the world but the Spirit who is from God, that we may understand what God has freely given us.

1 Corinthians 2:9–12, NIV

We see, then, that we cannot receive the revelation of what God has prepared for us through the mind or through the senses, but only through the spirit. God's Spirit, communicating directly with our spirits, the deepest, innermost secret part of us, gives us revelation. We enter into the understanding of truths we cannot apprehend in any other way.

God's Purpose for the Soul

The three main functions of the spirit—worship, fellowship, revelation—are God-related. The soul, according to most Bible interpreters, also has three main functions. We noted these earlier and observed the fact that they are all in the realm of self. These functions are the mind (or the intellect), the will and the emotions. Let's look at these briefly once more.

The Mind: "I Think"

The function of the soul in the area of the mind or the intellect is expressed in the simple phrase, *I think*. Two traits between the soul and the spirit may appear similar in this respect but they are quite different.

The spirit has direct revelation knowledge. It receives the truth from God, often in a supernatural way. The spirit says, "I know"; "I know God"; "I know I have eternal life"; "I know my sins are forgiven."

73

As one function of the soul, the mind deals with concepts, ideas, reasoning, problems and other mental processes.

Revelation belongs in the realm of the spirit; theology belongs in the realm of the mind. The spirit knows; the mind entertains ideas and reasons, and it shuffles around with concepts. In a certain sense, the mind is somewhat like a computer handling data.

The Will: "I Want"

The expression of the individual soul through the function of its will is this: "I want." In a certain sense, the expression of one's will determines the direction of that person's life. He or she may say, "I will believe" or "I won't believe"; "I will submit to God" or "I won't submit to God"; "I will love my neighbor" or "I won't love my neighbor."

We see quite a contrast between the spirit and soul in this respect. The spirit is not interested in self-expression; it expresses God. The soul expresses itself.

The Emotions: "I Feel"

The third area of the soul, the emotions, expresses itself in the simple little phrase, "I feel." The emotions respond to impressions from other functions of the soul and also from the body. Emotions are, therefore, in many cases unstable. Up one moment, down the next. Happy one moment, sad the next.

We see, again, the difference. The spirit responds to God, and God never changes. The soul responds to the world around it, and the world around it is in a continual state of flux. Because the soul is based on impressions it (along with the body) receives from the world, it is always subject to change. The soul may either respond to the spirit or rebuff the spirit.

The Soul's Purpose: Surrender

We can sum up the difference between spirit and soul with two key words.

The spirit must be *regenerated*. The spirit must have that particular kind of life that comes only from God. When Jesus said, "You must be born again," He was speaking about a spiritual experience. This is clear because, as we have noted, He went on to say immediately, "That which is born of the Spirit is spirit," contrasting it with physical birth. The rebirth is something that primarily affects man's spirit.

In contrast, the key word for the soul is that it must be *saved*. The soul is guilty. The soul has rebelled. The soul is the author of rebellion, and consequently God deals with the soul on that basis of rebellion. God says, in effect, "The penalty for your sin and your rebellion has been paid by the death of Jesus Christ on the cross. I'm offering you pardon and peace and reconciliation. But the only condition upon which you can receive it is that you lay down your rebellion."

For the soul, the key to salvation is to believe and then to surrender. It is important to understand that intellectual believing, without surrender, does not produce that radical change the soul needs. There are many, many people who have intellectual faith. They honestly, intellectually, believe the truth of the Gospel. They have never seen, however, that they are enemies and that the only way they can be reconciled with God is through surrender.

In World War II, when the Axis powers were facing defeat and surrender, they asked the Allies for the conditions of peace. The response of the Allies was, "We will make no conditions. We demand unconditional surrender." That is exactly how God answers the human soul when it wants peace. God says, "I'm not making any conditions. I demand unconditional surrender." Only through unconditional surrender can the soul be reconciled with God and have true peace and salvation.

God's Purpose for the Body

Now we come to God's program for the third element of the human personality: the body. In doing so, we immediately come up against a fact that has been prevalent in church history and theology. Christians have clung to an unscriptural tendency to underestimate the importance, the beauty, the significance and the glory of God's program for the body of the believer. The body is usually written off as something unworthy and evil.

The consensus has been that we almost need to be ashamed of our bodies, even to the point of trying to live as though, practically speaking, we do not have bodies. This tendency has, in some measure, been associated with a philosophy or outlook called asceticism, though I do not believe that all ascetics necessarily hold that view. Nonetheless, such a view does not accurately represent the way Scripture speaks about the human body.

The Body Was Formed by God

Let's look first at Psalm 139. In this passage, David, speaking to the Lord, marvels at the nature of his own body and praises God for it.

> For you created my inmost being; you knit me together in my mother's womb. I praise you because I am fearfully and wonderfully made; your works [specifically, his physical body] are wonderful, I know that full well. My frame [or my physical body] was not hidden from you when I was made in the secret place. When I was woven together in the depths of the earth, your eyes saw my

unformed body. All the days ordained for me were written in your book before one of them came to be.

Psalm 139:13–16, NIV

These are two beautiful words—*fearful* and *wonderful*. David tells us that the marvel of God's creation in the human body is fearful, "*awe-ful*," full of awe, awe-inspiring.

It blesses me to think that God had a secret place where He made our frame—that it was a kind of secret that He was keeping hidden until He could reveal it. In addition, David says that he was "woven together in the depths of the earth." That is a staggering thought. We read that at Creation God formed man of the dust, or the clay, so we know the physical body comes from the earth. But I understand David's words here to mean that God carefully prepared, in the earth, the various constituent elements that were going to form the human body.

God has a plan for the human body that originates in eternity. He carefully prepared the elements of its composition, and He has a program for every day of our lives. That is a staggering thought, isn't it? It should give us a very different concept of what our bodies mean to God.

The Body Has One Supreme Purpose

God designed the human body for one supreme purpose. If we fail to see this, we miss it all. The body of the regenerated believer is designed to be God's temple, God's dwelling place—the place where He lives. Paul states this clearly in First Corinthians:

> Do you not know that your body is a temple of the Holy Spirit, who is in you, whom you have received from God? You are not your own; you were bought at a price. Therefore honor God with your body.

1 Corinthians 6:19–20, NIV

It is important to understand that when Jesus bought us with His precious blood shed on the cross, He did not buy part of us. He bought us all—spirit, soul and body. He redeemed total humanity. He gave Himself totally that He might redeem us totally.

The body is included in redemption. And it is redeemed for a specific purpose—that it may be the special dwelling place, the temple of God, through the Holy Spirit. Almighty God, the only true God, indwells each sanctified believer in the physical body through the Holy Spirit.

Scripture gives us another important aspect to this truth. When Stephen spoke to the Jewish council accusing him he said: "The Most High does not dwell in houses made by human hands" (Acts 7:48, NASB).

God does not live in any physical temple. He does not live in a synagogue, a church, a chapel or any such place. He may visit those places when His people are there, but His dwelling place is the body of the redeemed believer. And there is a certain area in the body that God has set apart for the dwelling place of His Spirit. In Scripture, it is called the innermost part.

Let me just give you two passages that speak about this innermost part as the part of the body God particularly occupies. First, let's look at Proverbs 20:27, which we quoted earlier: "The spirit of man is the lamp of the LORD, searching all the innermost parts of his being" (NASB).

Clearly, the spirit dwells in the innermost parts of one's being. The Hebrew says, "the innermost chambers." But in the gospel of John, Jesus says something even more specific: "He who believes in Me, as the Scripture said, 'From his innermost being will flow rivers of living water.' But this He spoke of the Spirit, whom those who believed in Him were to receive" (John 7:38–39, NASB).

Jesus is talking about the place where the Holy Spirit will dwell in the believer. The above translation says, *from his innermost being.* The King James translation is much closer to the original. It says, *from his belly.* I could understand how people might think, *Well, the belly is somewhat vulgar and unrefined. We shouldn't talk about it in terms of sacred things.*

Interestingly enough, however, in the Greek language the same root word used here for *belly* is also used as the word for *heaven.* It means a hollow or concave place. Heaven, a concave place, is God's dwelling place in the physical universe. Heaven is God's dwelling place "out there." But somewhere in the innermost part of man, somewhere that we could perhaps call the belly, is a concave place where the Spirit of God dwells. Anyone who has experienced the power of the Spirit knows how the moving of the Spirit begins from that innermost part of your being.

The Body Is Meant for Righteous Living

Let's continue with another component of God's purpose for the body. Our physical members are to become slaves, or instruments, of righteousness. First the Holy Spirit takes up His dwelling place. Then our bodies become His instruments. Paul says,

> I am speaking in human terms because of the weakness of your flesh. For just as you presented your members as slaves to impurity and to lawlessness, resulting in further lawlessness, so now present your members [your physical members] as slaves to righteousness, resulting in sanctification [or holiness].
>
> Romans 6:19, NASB

God's program for our physical members is that we present them to Him as slaves, absolutely consigned to do His will. The King James Version says we present them to God, "as instruments," and by being offered in this way, they become sanctified. When presented to God without reservation, our bodies become sanctified and worthy temples of the Holy Spirit.

The Body Is God's Responsibility

Let me introduce one more vitally important fact about the body of the regenerated believer as God's temple. I will put it this way—simply and briefly: God accepts responsibility for the maintenance of His appointed temple.

When we offer our bodies to God without reservation, as a dwelling place for His Holy Spirit, He accepts full responsibility. When our members are yielded to Him without reservation as slaves or instruments to do His will, then God says, "All right, since the body is Mine, I'll accept responsibility for its maintenance and its well-being, both in this life and in the next."

Listen to what Paul says in his letter to the Romans:

> And if the Spirit of him who raised Jesus from the dead is living in you [notice, that is the basis: that the Holy Spirit is living in us, in our physical bodies], he who raised Christ from the dead will also give life to your mortal bodies through his Spirit, who lives in you.
>
> Romans 8:11, NIV

Notice, Paul is talking about our mortal bodies. Not only is he referring to the bodies we will have after resurrection, he is also talking about our bodies in this life.

Because our bodies have become the temples of the Holy Spirit, the Holy Spirit is dwelling in us. The same power is now living in our bodies that raised the dead body of Jesus from the tomb. God says that power will give life. It will impart vitality, vigor, strength and wholeness to our physical bodies.

Later, in chapters 11–13, we will discuss what our bodies will be like in the next world, but I will give you a short preview here. Philippians 3 describes the final transformation of our bodies at the return of the Lord:

> But our citizenship is in heaven. And we eagerly await a Savior from there, the Lord Jesus Christ, who, by the power that enables him to bring everything under his control, will transform our lowly bodies so that they will be like his glorious body.
>
> Philippians 3:20–21, NIV

That is the culmination of God's program for the body of the redeemed believer. At present, we have a lowly body. But when Jesus comes, if we are truly His, He will transform that lowly body into a glorious body that is like His own glorious body.

8

God's Plan of Control

In Him was life, and the life was the Light of
men.

John 1:4, NASB

All through the preceding chapters, we have been
looking together into the mirror of God's Word to
discover the real inner nature of man and see our
immense value in the eyes of the God who made us. Briefly,
I would summarize what we have seen with the following
brief statements.

First, a human being is a triune being, created in the likeness of a triune God. God is revealed as Father, Son and
Spirit—three Persons, one God. Man is revealed as spirit,
soul and body—three elements, but one personality.

Second, man's rebellion against God caused dislocation and malfunction of every area of his personality.

Third, through the miracle of regeneration, God has made provision for man's restoration in every area of his being. God has a plan for each area of the restored human personality— for the spirit, for the soul and for the body.

Fourth, we have observed that the three main functions of the regenerated spirit are all directly related to God. They are worship, fellowship and revelation. The three functions of the soul are all self-centered. They are mind, will and emotions, and in the process of regeneration, they are transformed. The function of the regenerated body is to be the temple of God, the dwelling place of God, the Holy Spirit. When the Holy Spirit takes residence in the temple, we are obligated to present our members to the Lord as slaves, or instruments, of God's purposes. As the body is yielded to the Holy Spirit, it becomes sanctified, or holy—set apart to God.

God's Plan for the Regenerated Person

In this chapter, I want to focus more closely on God's program to control regenerated man. This is a very, very important issue. Why? Because we may be regenerated, but if we do not understand how to function after regeneration, we may miss much of God's purpose for us. We may also miss many of the blessings God has for us.

Let me begin by saying that in God's plan, human personality is not a democracy. We so often hear the word *democracy* that we tend to think everything should function on that basis. God does not function on the basis of a democracy, and it is not His purpose that regenerated human personality should function on that basis.

God rules mankind, very definitely, from above through mankind's highest element—his spirit. The regenerated spirit of a person relates directly to God. The regenerated spirit is joined to the Lord, and through that spirit—through that link with God—God rules and directs the individual. We can, therefore, only be successful in this regenerated life insofar as our spirits are in contact with and yielded to God, and insofar as the remainder of our personalities are yielded to the direction of God.

That is God's purpose. Only insofar as His purpose and plan are worked out do we have success.

How It Works

To further illustrate this truth, let's take the example of David, through his spirit, exhorting his soul. We read of him doing so in Psalm 42. You will notice that David is speaking to his soul. This is not his soul speaking; it is his spirit speaking to his soul. The God-related part of him is speaking to the self-centered part of him.

> Why are you in despair, O my soul? And why have you become disturbed within me? Hope in God, for I shall yet praise Him, the help of my countenance and my God.
>
> Psalm 42:11, NASB

We see from this that the soul is moody. It is changeable, because it is related to itself and to the outside world. But the spirit that is related to God is not moody. It is not changeable. David is obviously in a mood, possibly a mood of despair. But his spirit says to his soul, "Come on, now. Shake yourself. It's time to praise the Lord. Don't give way to those moods."

In Psalm 103, we find the same concept. David says,

85

> Bless the LORD, O my soul [again, it is not his soul speaking, but his spirit], and all that is within me, bless His holy name. [You see, the spirit is always related to God. It always sees God as worthy to be praised.] Bless the LORD, O my soul, and forget none of His benefits; who pardons all your iniquities, who heals all your diseases; who redeems your life from the pit, who crowns you with lovingkindness and compassion; who satisfies your years with good things, so that your youth is renewed like the eagle.
>
> Psalm 103:1–5, NASB

Notice that the benefits of God, through the soul, reach also to the body. David speaks about the healing of our diseases and the prolonging of our youth. This is the way regenerated man is intended to function. The spirit of the person relates to God. The person's spirit then gives direction to the soul, and through the soul, divine direction, divine life and divine blessings flow out, even into the body.

Do you see the special responsibilities of each element of the human personality in this divine setup? First of all, the responsibility of the spirit is unbroken communion with God and worship toward God. Whenever there is any kind of separation between our spirits and God, then problems set in. The function of the spirit, therefore, is to maintain unbroken fellowship with God and to maintain worship at all times.

The function of the soul is submission and self-denial. Remember that it was in the soul that rebellion started. Through that problem, the soul has been infected with self-centeredness and self-assertion. It makes demands: "I want," "I think," "I feel," "I'm important" or "cater to me." Before we can function as God intends, that tendency has to be changed. The soul must surrender. You remember that Jesus said, "You have to deny yourself daily." Every day the soul has to say, "No, I will not assert myself. I will yield to the Spirit."

The Place of Self-Denial

Under God's control, the regenerated spirit guides the soul to embrace this self-denial. The words of Jesus again help us understand how this works: "Then Jesus said to His disciples, 'If anyone wishes to come after Me, he must deny himself, and take up his cross and follow Me'" (Matthew 16:24, NASB).

How do we follow Jesus? By denying ourselves. What does that mean? As we noted earlier, it means saying no to the self-interest of our souls. We understand now that it is the regenerated spirit that gives this direction.

My soul says, "I want." But my spirit responds, "No, what you want is not important. God's will takes precedence over yours."

My soul says, "I think." But my answer within my spirit is, "What you think is not important. What God says takes precedence over what you think."

My soul says, "I feel," and my spirit's answer to my soul is, "What you feel is not important. It is the revelation of God that is true. Your feelings are changeable and unreliable. That's why you are so moody. Snap out of it! It doesn't matter what you want. It doesn't matter what you think. It doesn't matter what you feel. I deny myself."

The passage continues with Jesus elaborating on this point: "For whoever wishes to save his life [soul] will lose it; but whoever loses his life [soul] for My sake will find it" (verse 25, NASB).

How can you lose your soul in order to find it? I understand it this way. You lay down that rebellious ego that is the soul. You renounce that kind of life that is in the soul. By this act, your soul willingly accepts death. It comes to the place of the cross and yields up its life. Then a totally new life is opened up to the soul—a life that flows from God, through the Spirit.

God's Preferred Dwelling

Let's look further now at the function of the body in this relationship. As we have already seen, the function of the regenerated body is to provide a pure temple for the Holy Spirit. Your body is to provide its yielded members as slaves to do the will of God, the Holy Spirit.

Let me say that I personally believe, in light of this mandate, that every believer has an obligation. That obligation is to keep your body in the best condition you can keep it in. It means always viewing your body as a temple of God, and your members as instruments of God. It is clear that God has a total commitment to dwell with man. To me that is one of the most astonishing facts of the Bible—that the Almighty God, the Creator, wants to dwell with man.

All through the Bible, God is planning it and arranging it. In the Greek of the New Testament, there is one particular word that means primarily a dwelling of God, and that is the word that appears more and more as we go into the New Testament. That word is *temple.*

God has had various temporary dwelling places: the Tabernacle of Moses, and the Temple of Solomon, which may well have been the most exquisite, glorious and costly building ever erected in the history of man. Although it was beautiful, it stood only a few brief years, and then it was destroyed because of the sin of the people.

In the New Testament, the revelation is that God is building a temple of living stones, and every believer is a stone in that temple. God dwells in that temple collectively by His Holy Spirit. But He also desires to dwell in the individual temple of the body of every believer.

Paul asks the question in 1 Corinthians 6:19: "Do you not know that your body is the temple of the Holy Spirit?" That, in a word, is the reason why we have a body.

God planned it all from eternity, including ongoing provision for these temples. Simply put, this provision is twofold. His Spirit dwells in our mortal bodies to impart life to them— His life. (See Romans 8:11.) The same power that raised the dead body of Jesus from the tomb dwells in our physical bodies right now.

His second provision is His Word. Psalm 107:20 says that God sent His Word and healed His people. His words are life to those who find them and health to all their flesh. If you put those two together, the Word and the Spirit, you have a complete picture of God's creative ability. The proof of that statement is Psalm 33:6: "By the word of the LORD the heavens were made, and all the host of them by the breath of His mouth [the Spirit]."

It only took God's Word and God's Spirit to bring the whole universe into being. And that same creative power is available to us because His Word and His Spirit are available to us.

Five Responsibilities for Our Bodies

How do we respond to the wonder of God's creation of our bodies? What are our responsibilities as believers? I believe there are five responsibilities we must consider.

First, we have to offer our bodies as living sacrifices on the altar of God's service.

Second, we need to present our bodies individually to the Lord to receive the Holy Spirit individually. (Collectively the temple is already indwelt. We have an obligation to provide the Lord with an individual, personal temple.)

Third, we are responsible to present our members, the parts of our bodies, as instruments of righteousness to God. Where the English says *instruments*, the Greek says *weapons*. That is rather interesting language. Your body—your members—are to be weapons that God can use in the war against sin and Satan.

89

Fourth, we have an obligation to keep the temple holy. In that regard the Bible specifically warns against fornication or sexual immorality. The Word says that the person who indulges in immorality is harming his own body.

Fifth, we owe it to ourselves to do some maintenance on the body. I have often remarked that it seems that many Christians are more faithful to maintain their cars than they are to maintain their bodies.

Based on my frequent teaching sessions on this topic, Ruth and I regularly make a proclamation concerning our bodies. We do it phrase by phrase. It is not just a ceremony; we believe this proclamation has tremendous spiritual significance. When you make this proclamation, you are accomplishing something very important in the unseen world. I would encourage you to make the following proclamation—phrase by phrase—with vigor and with faith. Are you ready?

> My body is a temple for the Holy Spirit, redeemed, cleansed and sanctified by the blood of Jesus. My members, the parts of my body, are instruments of righteousness yielded to God for His service and for His glory. The devil has no place in me, no power over me, no unsettled claims against me. All has been settled by the blood of Jesus. I overcome Satan by the blood of the Lamb and by the word of my testimony, and I love not my life unto the death. My body is for the Lord and the Lord is for my body.

If you really believe that, you have to thank Him. There is simply nothing else you can do. Why not take a moment right now to thank Him for the truth of that statement about your body?

Entirely, Completely Whole

In light of what I have pointed out so far, let's refer now to the prayer of Paul in 1 Thessalonians 5:23. We cited this prayer when we began our study of the triune man. This concept is so vital for a complete and perfect functioning of our personality that it bears repeating. This prayer expresses God's highest will for every human. Here is what Paul wrote:

> Now may the God of peace Himself sanctify you entirely; and may your spirit and soul and body be preserved complete, without blame at the coming of our Lord Jesus Christ.
>
> 1 Thessalonians 5:23, NASB

This is what it means for our whole being—spirit, soul and body—to be entirely sanctified and preserved complete.

I pointed out in earlier chapters that those two words, *entirely* and *complete*, indicate the total human personality as we understand it in the three elements of spirit, soul and body. God has a program by which each element of man and his total personality can be wholly sanctified and preserved blameless.

Let me finish this chapter by offering you a closing word of encouragement. It comes from the words of Paul in the very next verse: "Faithful is He who calls you, and He also will bring it to pass" (verse 24, NASB). It is in connection with this provision of God for complete holiness that Paul says, "God, who called you, is faithful, and He will bring it to pass."

If you do your part, you can be sure that God will do His.

9

Falling from Spiritual to Soulish

Their deeds will not allow them to return to their
God.

Hosea 5:4, NASB

I want you mentally to go back to what we discussed
earlier about how the serpent made his entrance. Remember what happened? Along came the serpent, and
he attacked the soul and severed the spirit from God's Spirit.
Fortunately, the new birth cut off the devil's impact on the soul
and renewed the spirit's relationship with the Spirit of God.

But suppose a person who is reborn does not maintain
the relationship with the Spirit of God. Suppose instead the
soul turns away again in rebellion toward Satan. Suppose the
soul responds to Satan's prompting. Have you discovered that
Satan does not give up the first time he tries his tactics? He
does not go very far away. He is right there waiting for the
next opportunity to inject something into your soul.

Suppose, then, a person has been born again but turns away from God in self-will and rebellion. Could that happen? Does it ever happen? It certainly does. When it happens, that person becomes soulish.

This is a word that we do not have in the English lexicon, and it is a tragedy that we do not. New Testament Greek uses two very important words that are not normally translated literally. I want to take a few moments to explain these words because they are the key to our understanding a tremendously important truth.

The adjective for the Greek word *pneuma* ("spirit") is *pneumatikos* ("spiritual"). The adjective for the Greek word *psuche* ("soul") is *psuchekos* and, really, the only correct translation is "soulish." Other languages, such as the Scandinavian languages—Danish, Swedish and Norwegian—have a word for "soulish," which we need desperately. Since English does not have a word that is formed from *soul* we have this made-up word, which I use frequently. But I find I have to explain it to people.

Here are some of the translations of *psuchekos* you will find in various versions of the Bible: "natural," "sensual," "carnal" or "worldly." But those translations obscure the fact that the same word is being used in different places. They also obscure the fact that the real problem is in the soul.

In this chapter, we are going to discuss people who are soulish. Such a person's spirit has been severed from connection with God. Now he still talks all the spiritual "talk." His name is still on the church roll. But his soul has turned back.

The Downward Spiral into Soulish

Let me begin by citing four passages in the New Testament, placements where this word *psuchekos* occurs. Interestingly,

you cannot find them in any concordance because the con-
cordances do not take you there. If you know how to use
other sources, you can get back behind the translation and
get to the original, but it is complicated. You could look
up *psuchekos* in these other sources and find it translated
"sensual," "natural," "worldly" and all sorts of things, but
that does not tell you what it is.

"A Natural Body"

The first passage I want to cite is 1 Corinthians 15:44, a
rather baffling verse. Talking about the body we will have
at resurrection, and the change that will come to us, it says
this: "It is sown [or buried] a natural body, it is raised a
spiritual body. There is a natural body, and there is a spiritual body."

Would you like to guess what the word *natural* is in Greek?
That's right. *Psuchekos*. It is sown a soulish body; it is raised
a spiritual body. Let me tell you what I understand that verse
to mean.

As I have said, our present bodies cannot be directly acti-
vated by the spirit. The spirit has to go through the soul. So,
you and I have a soulish body. When we get resurrected (and
this is exciting), we are going to have a spiritual body. Our
spirits are going to tell our bodies what to do and we are going
to do it. That is wonderful. You and I are going to be able to
go through doors and up and down—all of that. It will not
be a problem because we will have spiritual bodies.

"The Natural Man"

The second passage is in 1 Corinthians 2:11–14. These
are, by the way, important verses for those who are counsel-
ing others. Paul begins: "For what man knows the things of
a man except the spirit of the man which is in him? Even so

95

no one knows the things of God except the Spirit of God" (1 Corinthians 2:11).

You can only know the things of God from the Spirit of God. That knowledge comes down through your spirit. Paul continues: "Now we have received, not the spirit of the world, but the Spirit who is from God, that we might know the things that have been freely given to us by God" (verse 12). The only way we can know those things is by the Holy Spirit. It is revelation knowledge. "These things we also speak, not in words which man's wisdom teaches but which the Holy Spirit teaches, comparing spiritual things with spiritual" (verse 13).

Another translation for that last phrase is "unfolding spiritual truths to spiritual persons." In other words, you cannot communicate biblical truth in secular language. You cannot use the jargon of psychology or psychiatry adequately to impart spiritual truth. You have to use biblical terminology. That is why what we are studying in this section is critical— because you cannot ever really apprehend or communicate these truths until you learn to use the right words.

Then Paul goes on to say:

> The natural man [the soulish man] does not receive the things of the Spirit of God, for they are foolishness to him; nor can he know them, because they are spiritually discerned. But he who is spiritual judges all things, yet he himself is rightly judged by no one.
>
> 1 Corinthians 2:14–15

Here we come to the word *soulish*. The one who is in the realm of the soul and cut off from the spirit, the *natural* man, cannot know the things of God. In fact, they seem to him or her foolishness. So now you know, by the way, why some people make fun of legitimate spiritual practices like healing and speaking in tongues. You can understand their problem.

"Natural Wisdom"

The third passage I want to cite is a similar translation in the book of James:

> But if you have bitter jealousy and selfish ambition in your heart, do not be arrogant and so lie against the truth. This wisdom is not that which comes down from above, but is earthly, natural, demonic.
>
> James 3:14–15, NASB

The word *natural* there is literally *soulish*.

We see from this passage that there are two kinds of wisdom. There is one that comes down from above—from the Holy Spirit, through man's spirit, to the soul. That is pure wisdom. That is divine wisdom.

But there is another kind, when man's soul is not in submission to man's spirit. That wisdom is earthly, soulish, demonic. The word *earthly* indicates that there has been a degeneration. It is wisdom that has fallen far from the plane of direct relationship with God.

But it gets worse and worse. This Scripture presents a descending order of wisdom gained apart from God. First, it is earthly, then it is soulish and then it is demonic.

People ask, "How can Christians be exposed to demons?" This Scripture points toward one of the answers. When you get out of the spiritual relationship with God and go back into your soul relationship, it is earthly, soulish, and the soul is open to demons. Can you see this possibility? Wherever there is quarrel, strife and division, it is earthly, soulish, demonic. Could that be said of any churches?

When we get into the soulish realm, when the soul is not submitted to the spirit, but is still in pride and rebellion and self-assertion, it exposes us to demonic influences. And the kind of wisdom that results is not pure. It is not holy, but it is evil.

97

"Sensual Persons"

The fourth passage is in Jude. And notice, all these people are in the context of a church:

> These are grumblers, complainers, walking according to their own lusts [in other words, they have not said no to their souls]; and they mouth great swelling words, flattering people to gain advantage. But you, beloved, remember the words which were spoken before by the apostles of our Lord Jesus Christ: how they told you that there would be mockers in the last time who would walk according to their own ungodly lusts. These are sensual persons, who cause divisions, not having the Spirit.
>
> Jude 16–19

Again, can you guess what the word *sensual* is? Soulish. Who causes divisions in the church? Soulish persons. We see from this passage that the source of divisions among Christians lies in the realm of the soul.

When man is soulish—when he is no longer subject to his spirit and the Holy Spirit—that is when division, strife, quarreling, heresy and all sorts of evils come in. The soul that is not submitted to the spirit is unprotected and uncovered. It is exposed to evil influences—both fleshly and demonic.

How critical it is for us to be able to discern these things! We must be able to see the difference between the spiritual and the soulish. My honest comment is that most Christians I have met are not able to discern. They are continually fooled by something soulish that passes itself off as spiritual. I believe the main activity of the soulish is to produce a substitute for the real thing.

Recognizing the Difference

We discussed in chapter 7 three main functions of the human spirit—worship, fellowship and revelation. In order to help you discern the differences between spiritual and soulish, let's review here two of those, worship and revelation, and observe, first, the proper place of soul and body in relation to them in the regenerated individual. Then we will follow with examples of what soulish substitutes might look like.

Worship

Worship is the activity by which the regenerated individual is united with God. That is why I believe worship is the highest activity of a human being. If you do not see worship that way, you may not understand enough about worship. You need to see how creative worship is. Just as union is procreative in the physical, so it is in the spiritual. I do not believe the Church is ever really productive until it worships. It is by worship that we unite with God's Spirit. It is out of worship that creativity proceeds. Jesus said that the Father is looking for those who will worship in spirit and in truth (see John 4:23–24).

What is the activity in the soul that corresponds to worship in the regenerated individual? Some might say prayer, and that is a good answer, but prayer is all embracing. Praise is the better answer. Remember the words of the virgin Mary: "My soul magnifies the Lord, and my spirit has rejoiced in God my Savior" (Luke 1:46–47). You cannot mix those two up. They are different.

What does the body do in worship? I would say bow or kneel—any physical expression. We could also prostrate ourselves, clap our hands or lift our hands. Since we are total human beings, every part of our person should be appropriately involved in worship.

Revelation

Regarding the other topic for comparison, revelation, Paul prays "that the God of our Lord Jesus Christ, the Father of glory, may give to you the spirit of wisdom and revelation in the knowledge of Him" (Ephesians 1:17).

Revelation is something that comes directly from the Spirit of God to your spirit. It does not go through your soul.

What would be the action corresponding to revelation in the area of the soul? I would say teaching, doctrine or theology. These are a matter of reasoning. Incidentally, most of the Church has a lot of theology and no revelation.

In regard to revelation, what do we have in the realm of the body? The answer I would give is sense perception. With your senses you perceive the natural world.

Soulish Substitutes

I want to look now at some suggested soulish substitutes for this genuine spiritual behavior. This list, again, is entirely subjective; it is my understanding.

First of all, take *worship*. What is the soulish behavior that takes the place of worship? My answer is *entertainment*. I think the majority of Christians cannot distinguish between music that is entertainment and music that is worship. Much of the responsibility lies at the door of Nashville. For the sake of a lot of dollars, they commercialize religious music to the point where people look to it for entertainment. Worship is not entertainment. Entertainment is getting for yourself. Worship is giving to God.

Next is *revelation*. This is very subjective for me because of experiences I have been through. You may not have been through the same things. The substitute here is *manipulation*. I think of circumstances like this one. You are in a meeting and the preacher says, "Now, there are ten people here tonight, each of whom is going to give a thousand dollars." Is that a revelation? It could be. But if it is not a revelation, then what is it? Manipulation.

I have a Swiss friend who is a businessman. He told me that he went to a meeting like that. The preacher made the request and he gave a thousand dollars. He went home kicking himself all the way. He knew he had been manipulated. His wife said to him, "If I had done that, you would have gotten angry with me."

The exact terminology is not the point here. I simply want to awaken you to the difference between the spiritual and the soulish. I want you to see this for your own survival. It is essential that you learn to distinguish between them. When you understand the concept, you can discern the differences fairly easily.

Take the spiritual act of *discernment*. What is the soulish replacement? It is *criticism*. Soulish people are critical.

What about *conviction*? Most people would not get the substitute, but it is one of my pet peeves. My answer is *guilt*. It is my strong belief that the Holy Spirit never makes you feel guilty. He will convict you of sin, tell you what you have done wrong, call you to repentance. And when you have repented, the matter is finished.

I have learned to be extremely suspicious of people who make me feel guilty. Usually they are trying to manipulate me. You see, with guilt the matter is never settled. *Did I do enough? Should I have done more? What did I say? Should I have said something different?* It is never over.

How about *compassion*? The spurious soulish alternative in my terminology is *sympathy*. A lot of people want sympathy, but they do not want compassion. Compassion is powerful, but it mandates change. It says, "You can be changed." Sympathy says, "Poor you. I'll sit down with you and sympathize with you. I'll feed your self-pity."

The Battleground for the Believer

Do you see how the main problem area is always the soul? Rebellion of the soul is the root cause of all human problems.

We cannot afford not to be on our guard. Since this is the area Satan targets, you and I can be sure we will be tested in the area of the soul.

The soul is the area of ongoing temptation. Because an element of disobedience has infected the soul of unregenerate man, we no longer have to be tempted from outside. Temptation finds its source within each one of us, making it far too easy to respond to the evil that is outside. It occurs in all three areas of the soul—in the mind, the will and the emotions. If you analyze your problems as a Christian, you find that the soul area is where they all start.

Since the soul was created from the union of the inbreathed Spirit from above with the dust or clay that came from the ground, you can see a kind of built-in potential for tension in us as human beings. There is something in us from above and there is something in us from beneath. You have most likely experienced that tension—where one part of you wants to go up and another part is pulling you down. The philosopher Plato described it this way: The chariot of the soul has two horses, one white and one black. The white horse wants to go upward; the black horse wants to go downward. That is a figurative picture, but I believe it is the truth.

The human soul is really the battleground of tremendous spiritual forces. When you understand that truth, you will not feel condemned if at times you find yourself in a battle. In fact, all of us find ourselves in a battle. We need to understand not only the nature of that battle but also God's provision for victory.

Safety and victory lie in maintaining a God-appointed relationship. We will inevitably have pressures and temptations, but as long as that proper relationship is maintained, we will ultimately always have safety and victory.

If, however, the soul turns to self-will and rebellion, then it becomes exposed to sin and to Satan. The downward slide begins. In a certain sense, sin is failure to function according to the purpose for which we were created. Salvation from sin restores to us the possibility to function in that way.

Do you understand the essence of what I am saying here? The *only* safety for human personality is for the soul to be in continual submission and self-denial, yielded to the spirit, and the spirit in turn related to God. There and there alone is safety.

The Test for Soulish Behavior

What is the ultimate test? How do we know if someone is spiritual or soulish? By his or her fruit.

We read this in Scripture at the end of the Sermon on the Mount. Jesus, in His wisdom, says, in effect, "Beware of false prophets, who come to you nicely dressed as sheep and inwardly they are wolves." How will you know them? "You will know them by their fruits" (Matthew 7:16). Check the fruit, my friend. Don't just listen to the language. The one who is soulish cannot receive revelation from God. The one who is spiritual naturally receives revelation from God.

A passage that we referred to earlier, Hebrews 4:12–13, seems to indicate that the only thing that will divide between soul and spirit is the Word of God. If we go to any other source, we will not get an answer. I believe the only people who can understand this truth are the people who go to God's Word and look in that mirror.

10

Entire Sanctification

You have dealt well with Your servant, O
LORD, according to Your word. Teach me good
judgment and knowledge, for I believe Your
commandments.

Psalm 119:65–66

As I understand it, and as I have pointed out before, God never ceased caring about Adam and his descendants. This is one of the amazing facts of history— and evidence of how valuable we are to our Creator.

We mentioned this in chapter 2, quoting James 4:5: "[God] jealously desires the Spirit which He has made to dwell in us" (NASB). God breathed a little of Himself in us, and He has never given up on us. He has never said, "Good-bye. I abandon you." For thousands of years He has been jealously craving a renewed relationship with that spirit. As Luke 19:10 affirms, Jesus came "to seek and to save that which was lost." That which God had imparted into man had been separated, cut off and, as it were, carried away on the tide of rebellion.

Just before the Jewish leaders procured Jesus' crucifixion, the high priest said about Jesus that it was profitable for the nation that one man should die rather than all the people should perish. John comments that the high priest further prophesied that Jesus "would gather together in one the children of God who were scattered abroad" (John 11:52). I believe that this verse refers to God's passionate desire to gather back that which was scattered and lost. Jesus came for that purpose.

The New Creation

Let's look at this new creation just for a few moments. This is the most glorious revelation. Paul says, "Therefore, if anyone is in Christ, he is a new creation; old things have passed away; behold, all things have become new. Now all things are of God" (2 Corinthians 5:17–18).

The new creation is entirely of God. It is totally new. God does not patch us up. He does not repair us. He does not improve us. He makes a new creation in Christ. Only God can do that because He is the Creator.

The way this happens is vividly described in the gospel of John, the resurrection appearance of Jesus to His disciples. Jesus appears behind closed doors and says,

> "Peace be with you." When He had said this, He showed them His hands and His side [proving that it was the same body they had seen crucified]. Then the disciples were glad when they saw the Lord. So Jesus said to them again, "Peace be to you! As the Father has sent

Me, I also send you." And when He had said this, He breathed on them, and said to them, "Receive the Holy Spirit."

John 20:19–22

The Greek wording for this command could equally well be translated, "Receive holy breath." It was the Holy Spirit, and He was breathed into them.

If you consider the original creation, here is the exact counterpart in the new creation. The resurrected Savior, the totally victorious Christ, meets His disciples and breathes into them a totally new kind of life, a life that has triumphed over sin, death, hell, the grave and Satan. A totally undefeatable life. That is what it is to be born again. That is what it is to be a Christian. It is to meet the resurrected Jesus and receive from Him divine, eternal resurrection life.

At that point, the disciples passed out of Old Testament salvation into New Testament salvation. Old Testament salvation looks forward; New Testament salvation looks back to an accomplished historical fact. To enter into New Testament salvation, Paul says we have to do two things: confess Jesus as Lord and believe that God has raised Him from the dead (see Romans 10:9).

The disciples had already confessed Jesus as Lord. This appearance was the first moment that they believed that God had raised Jesus from the dead. As Peter says, they were begotten again (see 1 Peter 1:3). They entered into salvation through a new birth.

The Truths We Know

Our focus in this book has been on this basic question of discovering our true value, and how this knowledge helps us grow in the life God intends for His children. I have stated my conviction that the Bible is the only book that not only asks

107

this question, but also provides a satisfying answer to it. I trust that as we study the nature of man, it is becoming clearer and clearer to you why you matter so much to God.

What is our identity? To answer that question we are learning that we must know how we—creations of spirit, soul and body—are designed to function, both in relationship to God Himself and to each other. This is a matter of great practical importance for every born-again believer. It gives us direction on how God intends us to live in this new life. It helps us know who we are.

Let's review what we have learned thus far.

Over the previous chapters, I have explained that the Bible serves as a mirror that shows us our inner nature. In a normal, physical mirror, we can look at our outward appearance, but the Bible is a spiritual mirror. This mirror reveals that we are triune beings created in the likeness of a triune God.

The revelation of the triune God, which we receive in the same mirror of God's Word, is that God is Father, Son and Spirit—three Persons, one God. We have understood that God created us in His likeness, so the reflection of total man in God's Word reveals three related elements—spirit, soul and body. These came into being at Creation when the Spirit of God, from above, was breathed into the body of clay below. The union of spirit and clay, or spirit and body, produced a living soul.

God relates to us primarily through our spirits. The chain of authority in human personality comes down from God through the Holy Spirit, to the human spirit, to the human soul, to the human body.

We also covered the particular appropriate functions of each element of man. The primary responsibility of the spirit is unbroken communion and worship with God. As long as the spirit remains in relationship with God, we are centered in the right way. The function of the soul is submission and self-denial. And the function of the body is to provide the Spirit with a pure temple and with yielded members.

We also traced how at the Fall we turned away from God in rebellion, with disastrous effects on every element of our being. Mankind's spirit died—we became spiritually dead in sin. Our souls were infected with rebellion. Our bodies became subject to corruption, decay, sickness, old age and ultimately, death.

Thank God that He provided a remedy for this terrible condition! God's remedy is regeneration—being reborn. Through faith in Jesus Christ, His atoning death and resurrection, we have these four effects of salvation or the new birth in each area of life.

First of all, the new birth imparts new life to the spirit. We are born again. Our spirits are no longer dead in trespasses and sins.

Second, the new birth restores the spirit's contact with God. The separation between us and God is taken away.

Third, it releases our souls from Satan's control. Satan's influence on the soul is canceled.

Fourth, it restores God's program of relationship, which is from top to bottom.

The Exciting Future

The underlying theme of all we have discussed is how valuable God considers us, how precious we are to Him, how much we matter to Him. I hope the truths we have examined are helping you discover your true value and identity in God's eyes.

And yet with all we have learned, there is yet more than we can ever comprehend. Scripture says, "Eye has not seen, nor ear heard, nor have entered into the heart of man the things which God has prepared for those who love Him" (1 Corinthians 2:9). In the final three chapters we will venture into the changes that we will experience upon Christ's return.

11

The Climax of Life's Destiny

The world is passing away, and the lust of it; but
he who does the will of God abides forever.

1 John 2:17

We are heading toward the grand conclusion of our understanding of how much we matter to God.

In regard to the title of this chapter, "The Climax of Life's Destiny," I first of all want to say that God is not the god of the anticlimax. This age is not going to end with an anticlimax, contrary to what some people may think. God has an exciting plan, a most amazing event that will complete the redemption of our spirits, souls and bodies. In this chapter we will see how that event will take place.

As a student at Eton and Cambridge, I was a great admirer of the poet T. S. Eliot. (Later in his life, incidentally, he became a very devout Anglican.) One of his poems called "Preludes" contains these lines:

> The worlds revolve like ancient women
> Gathering fuel in vacant lots.

Let me simply state: That is not how it is going to be. The end is not going to drift to a dreary anticlimax. It is going to come to a tremendous climax.

If you consider the writing in the Bible, God has a tremendous sense of theater. Think of the dramatic events described there. Think of Elijah challenging the prophets of Baal by declaring, "The God who answers by fire, let him be God." The prophets of Baal spend all day frantically employing all their occult practices, with absolutely no results. Then, in the evening, Elijah moves forward. He straightens up the altar. He pours water over it three times to make sure it is totally nonflammable. And then, down comes the fire! All the people fall on their faces before this amazing display of God's power. That is drama. That is not an anticlimax.

Think of some of the scenes from the ministry of Jesus. He stands in front of the tomb of Lazarus, who has been dead four days. With a loud voice, Jesus commands: "Lazarus, come out!" A moment later, what was previously a corpse, still with the grave clothes around his face and his body, shuffles out! Can you think of anything more dramatic than that?

Think of the resurrection. The women go to the tomb and find it empty. All of them leave, except Mary Magdalene. I believe Mary must have been the one who, in a way, loved the Lord the deepest. She simply cannot tear herself away. (I can never think of this without weeping.) She turns and sees a figure. But she does not bother to look closely because she thinks He is the gardener. She says, "If you have taken Him away, tell me where you have laid Him." And Jesus says, "Mary." She gasps, "Rabboni!" It always blesses me that He has not ascended to the Father at that time. Jesus must know the terrible agony in her heart and makes sure to comfort her before He even ascends to the Father.

The Bible is full of drama. Believe me, God is going to bring this present age to a dramatic conclusion. It is going to be orchestrated. All heaven and earth are going to be involved. The Bible says that when the time comes for the Marriage Supper of the Lamb, everybody in heaven and on earth will be singing "Hallelujah!"

You might say that we see a certain foreshadowing of this excitement and drama building in various events we ourselves can witness. Here is a personal example. Ruth and I had an exciting wedding. Initially, we had intended to get married very quietly—just a few members of the family, about forty people. Well, it got out of hand. We could not keep people away. The wedding party alone was forty people.

More than six hundred people attended. It was a combined Jewish/Christian ceremony, and that concept alone meant a lot of drama. You may not be aware of this detail, but in a Jewish wedding ceremony, at a certain moment, the bridegroom first offers a cup of wine to the bride and then he himself drinks the rest. Together they drain the contents of the cup. Then he puts the glass under his foot and crushes it. When I did that at our wedding, the whole place burst into applause. Utterly spontaneous.

Do you see that God is not dull? He is not inactive. If you think the age is going to be dull when it ends, you are going to be in for a surprise.

Seeking Even More Than Heaven!

When God brings the age to a close and mankind's redemption is complete, all three elements of the human personality will be complete. Our redemption is not fully worked out until the body has been redeemed.

Contrary to popular belief, the end of the Christian life is not to get to heaven. That is where most Christians stop in their thinking. Heaven is only a stage in the process. The end of the Christian life is for the spirit, soul and body to be reunited in a totally new body. That is the end. That is what we are looking forward to. If you are just looking forward to getting to heaven, you have not seen to the end of the journey.

Look at the beautiful words of the apostle Paul in his letter to the Philippians. I believe these are some of the most glorious words in the New Testament. I never read them without being inspired and challenged.

> Yet indeed I also count all things loss for the excellence of the knowledge of Christ Jesus my Lord, for whom I have suffered the loss of all things, and count them as rubbish, that I may gain Christ and be found in Him, not having my own righteousness, which is from the law, but that which is through faith in Christ, the righteousness which is from God by faith; that I may know Him and the power of His resurrection, and the fellowship of His sufferings, being conformed to His death, if, by any means, I may attain to the resurrection from the dead. Not that I have already attained, or am already perfected; but I press on, that I may lay hold of that for which Christ Jesus has also laid hold of me. Brethren, I do not count myself to have apprehended; but one thing I do, forgetting those things which are behind and reaching forward to those things which are ahead, I press toward the goal for the prize of the upward call of God in Christ Jesus.
>
> Philippians 3:8–14

What was Paul's objective? There is not a word in this passage about going to heaven. Do you understand? When you die your spirit and your soul will go to heaven, but your body will be laid in a tomb or grave of some sort. That is not the end. The end is when your body's redemption is complete, and it is united again, perfected, with your spirit and your soul. So Paul presses on "if, by any means, I may attain to the resurrection from the dead" (verse 11). What was his objective? What was his goal? Not heaven, but resurrection.

The word used there is used in only that one place in the entire New Testament. The word is *exanastasis*. *Ex* means "out of," so this refers to the resurrection "out of" the dead. It is not the resurrection of all the dead. It is a preliminary resurrection of only the righteous dead, the true believers. That was Paul's objective—that he may attain to that resurrection.

Let's turn to the book of Revelation for a moment, and the concept of resurrections. One resurrection has already taken place: the resurrection of Jesus. There remain two: the resurrection of true believers and then, subsequently, the resurrection of the remaining dead.

> But the rest of the dead did not live again [did not come to life again] until the thousand years were finished. This [meaning those who were resurrected at the beginning of the thousand years] is the first resurrection. Blessed and holy is he who has part in the first resurrection.
>
> Revelation 20:5–6

Paul in Philippians is talking about the goal of being among those in the first resurrection, the "out of" resurrection. This does not include all the dead, but is a resurrection of the true believers out from among the dead.

Do you want to be one of those people? Blessed and holy?

The Bible gives several beautiful pictures of the resurrection, but I think one of the most exciting is in 1 Thessalonians. (Actually, the resurrection or the coming of the Lord is the theme of both 1 and 2 Thessalonians.)

Paul is here relating a revelation—something that was made known to him supernaturally by the Spirit of God. It was something that could not be known just by reasoning or even by studying the Old Testament Scriptures. Paul says,

> For this we say to you by the word of the Lord, that we who are alive and remain until the coming of the Lord [the Greek word here is *parousia*, the standard Greek word for the coming of the Lord] will by no means precede those who are asleep.
>
> 1 Thessalonians 4:15

We will not precede them in resurrection, you understand, or in meeting the Lord: The resurrection is coincident with the return of the Lord. It is the Lord Himself, and only He, who can bring about the resurrection.

Now we come to these dramatic words. Again, I want to emphasize that this is not going to be an anticlimax:

> For the Lord Himself will descend from heaven with a shout, with the voice of an archangel, and with the trumpet of God. And the dead in Christ [not the rest of the dead, but those who died in faith in Jesus] will rise first. Then we who are alive [believers who are alive on earth at that time] and remain shall be caught up together with them in the clouds to meet the Lord in the air. And thus we shall always be with the Lord. Therefore comfort one another with these words.
>
> 1 Thessalonians 4:16–18

The word *comfort* is from the same word that gives us *paraclete*, which is one of the titles of the Holy Spirit. It really has two meanings, and "comfort" does not define it completely. It covers one of its meanings, but not the other. This word means "to cheer up," but it also means "to stir up." Certainly if people are sad and down, you cheer them up. But if they are lazy and backslidden, you stir them up. It is a ministry of the Holy Spirit either way. The Bible says clearly that we are to cheer one another up and to stir one another up with this revelation.

Without belaboring the point, I would like to ask you a question. Have you really been cheered up or stirred up by hearing this message in your church? In most settings when I have asked this question, usually there is not one person who has responded. I believe this pinpoints a tremendous lack in the Church of Jesus Christ. This tremendous truth, which is the great encouragement for Christian living, has almost dropped out of preachers' vocabularies. This is a tragic loss for the Church.

The Dramatic Element

Now let's examine the exciting details of the event Paul describes. First of all, the Lord is coming back. Does that make you want to say "Amen"? (Go ahead and do it.) Jesus is coming back in person. It is not going to be a Messianic age as some forms of Judaism teach. It will be the Messiah Himself.

We will look at three Scriptures on this theme, all of which relate to 1 Thessalonians 4, so keep that passage in mind. The first passage is in the gospel of John. These are the words of Jesus Himself as He is bidding farewell to His disciples. Jesus says, "And if I go and prepare a place for you, I will come again and receive you to Myself; that where I am, there you may be also" (John 14:3).

That is very simple. Even a child can understand that. "I will come again." Do you believe that? I do.

The second passage is the testimony of the angels in the book of Acts. Jesus has just ascended in a cloud and the apostles are standing there, I believe, straining their heads upward to see if they can catch one more glimpse of the Lord. As they stand there with their heads up, two men in white appear by them who are angels. They say, "Don't waste any more time looking up, because that's not going to be what happens next." Then they say this: "Men of Galilee, why do you stand gazing up into heaven? This same Jesus, who was taken up from you into heaven, will so come in like manner as you saw Him go into heaven" (Acts 1:11).

Notice the phrase *this same Jesus*. Tremendous emphasis is given to the fact that it will be the Lord in person who will be coming back. And He is coming back in the same way He left. Two features here are, I think, obvious: First, He went in the clouds; He is coming back in the clouds. Second, He went from the Mount of Olives; He is coming back to the Mount of Olives. That is where His feet will rest on earth.

Then for the third passage we return to 1 Thessalonians: "For the Lord Himself will descend" (1 Thessalonians 4:16).

Do you see the significance of these three passages? Jesus says, "I." The angels say, "This same Jesus." Paul says, "The Lord Himself." The Bible is very, very careful to emphasize that this is not to be just a different age. This is the personal return of the Son of God in glory and in power.

A Noisy Event

This dramatic event is going to be accompanied by three noises. First Thessalonians 4:16 says, "The Lord Himself will descend from heaven with a shout, with the voice of an archangel, and with the trumpet of God."

First will be the shout of the Lord. Did you know that God shouts? He does not always speak in a soft voice. There is quite a lot in Isaiah about the Lord getting angry and shouting. Second will be a proclamation by an archangel. And third will be a trumpet.

We need to consider each of these three sounds, realizing that they will be the sounds accompanying this event.

The Voice of Jesus

Here is Jesus' description of the event:

"Do not marvel at this; for the hour is coming in which all who are in the graves [those who have been actually buried] will hear His voice and come forth—those who have done good, to the resurrection of life [that is the first resurrection], and those who have done evil, to the resurrection of condemnation [that is the second, subsequent resurrection]."

John 5:28–29

Did you notice in that passage what brings the dead out of the tombs? It is the voice of the Lord. He is the only One who can call the dead back out of their graves. Jesus raised three people from death in His ministry. In each case, He was careful to specify the individual who was to come back. Why? Because who knows what would have happened if He had not named the person.

When He raised the little daughter of Jairus, He said, "Young girl, I'm talking to you. You come back" (see Mark 5:22–24, 35–43). And immediately she came back. When Jesus met the widow of Nain coming out of the city with her son— her only son—on the funeral bier, He stopped the bier and said, "Young man, I say to you arise" (see Luke 7:11–17). And he rose. Then as Jesus stood outside the tomb of Lazarus, He said, "Lazarus, come out" (see John 11:1–44). If Jesus had not specified Lazarus, all the dead would have walked out!

Jesus is the only one who has the authority to raise the dead. It is His voice alone that can bring the dead out of the tomb. When He comes, I do not know what He is going to say—perhaps *My redeemed people* or *My true believers, you come out*. And we will come out.

The Angel and the Trumpet

One of the other sounds we mentioned will be the proclamation of an archangel. Most Bible commentators believe the archangel will be Gabriel, simply because it seems to be his job to proclaim interventions of God in human history.

The last of the sounds is the trumpet. I find that I get shudders when I think about that trumpet. To me, a trumpet is a

119

very special instrument. A trumpet kind of blasts you out of your complacency. It is a rather military musical instrument.

Paul talks about the trumpet as well. Let's look at what he says in 1 Corinthians 15. This chapter deals with the resurrection, and it is one of the longest chapters of the New Testament. Paul says in these verses, "Behold, I tell you a mystery [a hidden truth that is now revealed]: We shall not all sleep [that is, in death]" (verse 51).

You see, the believer sleeps when he dies, because he is going to wake up again. It is not permanent. That word is never used of unbelievers in death. Only of believers. Paul continues: ". . . but we shall all be changed—in a moment, in the twinkling of an eye" (verses 51–52).

Do you know what that phrase means? As long as it takes to blink will be as long as it takes for this change. Do you know why you will blink? Because a brilliant light will strike your eyes, you will not be able to keep your eyelids open. In that instant, you will turn and look at the person next to you, and that person next to you will be totally different. At that moment there is going to be an instantaneous, total change of the physical body of every believer.

Paul goes on to say: "For the trumpet will sound, and the dead will be raised incorruptible, and we shall be changed" (verse 52). That declaration is exactly in line with 1 Thessalonians 4.

Revelation talks about a number of trumpets, but I think the one referred to here has to be the last trumpet. I cannot think of anything that will follow this in the way of trumpets. I may be wrong, but that seems to be logical. And I believe strongly in logic.

Is This the Rapture?

This dramatic event we have been discussing is commonly referred to as the Rapture. A lot of clever people have been telling Christians that there is no such word as *rapture* in the New Testament. I find that rather naïve, because the New Testament was not written in English. In fact, you will not find any English words in the New Testament. It is a question of what translation is used. The word we are talking about is *harpazo*. This word means "to snatch, to grab, to pull up."

There is no English word formed from that verb; a Latin verb is used to translate it. This is this word *rapio*, which means exactly the same as *harpazo*. There is a noun formed from it, and also a verb, which is *rapture*. We see that, in actual fact, it is a perfectly accurate way to describe what Paul is talking about. I believe there is a certain prejudice in some quarters against the Rapture because some people cannot believe that something like it will really happen. But I believe it.

To Be Snatched Away

Just to make this clear, this word *harpazo* is used somewhere around a dozen times in the New Testament. I want to show you some of the places where it is used so you can form your own opinion as to what it really means.

Let's turn, first of all, to Jesus' parable of the sower and its interpretation. Jesus says concerning the seed that is sown by the wayside: "When anyone hears the word of the kingdom, and does not understand it, then the wicked one comes and snatches away what was sown in his heart" (Matthew 13:19). The word here for "snatch away" is *harpazo*.

In the gospel of John, we find Jesus' parable of the good shepherd: "But a hireling [a hired man], he who is not the shepherd, one who does not own the sheep, sees the wolf coming and leaves the sheep and flees; and the wolf catches the sheep and scatters them" (John 10:12). The verb He uses

121

to describe catching the sheep is *harpazo*. It is quick. It is forceful. And it changes the total situation instantly.

Going on with other Scriptures, we come to 2 Corinthians. Paul is talking here about a certain man who had a marvelous supernatural experience:

> I know a man in Christ who fourteen years ago—whether in the body I do not know, or whether out of the body I do not know, God knows—such a one was caught up to the third heaven. . . . he was caught up into Paradise.
>
> 2 Corinthians 12:2–4

Can you guess what word is used here for being caught up? *Harpazo*. You can readily see that the meaning is consistent all the way through.

Another Scripture is Jude 23. This verse talks about people who have been believers and gotten themselves into very dangerous spiritual situations. The writer says, "Save [them] with fear, pulling them out of the fire."

What do you think the word is here for pulling them out? *Harpazo*. Do you see how consistent this is? The word is to reach out, grab something and pull it to yourself. It is quick. It is sudden. It is forceful. And it totally changes the situation. That is what *rapture* is.

This is also what happened to Philip after he baptized the Ethiopian eunuch: "Now when they came up out of the water, the Spirit of the Lord caught Philip away, so that the eunuch saw him no more" (Acts 8:39). Philip was caught away—*harpazo*.

Does This Still Happen?

Is *rapture* simply a biblical term, describing instances affecting either the early Church or the coming future of the Church? Does it have any significance for us in our daily lives?

Let me tell you of two instances known to me. One took place with Brother David du Plessis, who has gone to be with the Lord. I once heard him say that he came out of a meeting in a certain city in South Africa, and he realized that he was supposed to be in another meeting on the other side of the city at that same time. David closed his eyes to pray and when he opened his eyes, he was outside the place of the other meeting.

The other occurrence is even more remarkable. It happened in Zambia to a missionary couple that Ruth and I know very well. They are tremendously faithful servants of the Lord who have really worked themselves to the bone in the cause of Christ. They were driving at night in a car, pulling a trailer along the very dusty, uneven roads of Zambia. They were very tired, and they came to a place they recognized on the road. They knew from that point that they had 25 more miles to go to get where they were going. At that point they closed their eyes and prayed just briefly. And when they opened their eyes, they, the car and the trailer were all at their destination. We must not underestimate what God can do. What these individuals experienced is called "translation power."

And here is a natural example, an interesting fact from natural science. A close friend of ours is an Israeli young woman who worked for us for five years. She happens to be a bird watcher, and a very professional one at that. She told us that at certain seasons of the year, huge numbers of birds migrate through Israel.

Did you know that some fifteen million birds fly south and north once each year in Israel? They come from Russia, from Europe, from Western Europe. As they migrate south, they cannot make it all the way to Africa. So somewhere near Eilat they land. The bird watchers there catch them, put bands on their legs and let them go so that people can check where those birds end up.

Our friend told us that some of the birds that land at Eilat are in a bird family called raptors. Do you know what a raptor is? It is a bird that swoops down over its prey, picks it up with its claws or its beak and carries it off. Even in nature, the image is absolutely consistent. Honestly, to say that *rapture* is the wrong word to describe the gathering up of the Church at the end is actually to display ignorance.

One Consistent Meaning

To close this chapter, I want to give just one more example from the book of Revelation. Here we read about the woman in the wilderness: "She bore a male Child who was to rule all nations with a rod of iron. And her Child was caught up to God and His throne" (Revelation 12:5).

By now you can guess what word is used to describe being caught up: *harpazo*.

Can you agree with me that this has one consistent meaning all the way through the New Testament? So when Paul says "we shall be caught up," there is no scriptural reason to doubt what it means.

It will be sudden. It will be swift. It will be extremely powerful. And it will totally change our situation. Can you end this chapter by thanking God with me for the Rapture that is to take place? Now, let's see how different we will be when that event takes place.

12

We Shall Be Changed

"We give You thanks, O Lord God Almighty, the
One who is and who was and who is to come. . . .
[You] reward Your servants the prophets and the
saints, and those who fear Your name, small and
great."

Revelation 11:17–18

hen we discover the remarkably dramatic event
God has planned for us, we realize how truly
valuable and special we are to God. We matter
so much to the Lord that He intends to prepare us to spend
eternity with Him.

In the preceding chapter, we saw how the Lord intends to
complete the redemption process in our spirits, souls and
bodies. In this chapter, we will discuss the scope and extent
of the change God will bring to our total person.

The Change We Will Experience

Let's look in this section at the change that is going to take place in us. In 1 Corinthians 15:42 and following, Paul is talking about the resurrection of the dead. He is answering this question: What kind of a body will we have?
Paul says,

> So also is the resurrection of the dead. The body is sown in corruption, it is raised in incorruption. It is sown in dishonor, it is raised in glory. It is sown in weakness, it is raised in power. It is sown a natural body, it is raised a spiritual body. There is a natural body, and there is a spiritual body.
>
> verses 42–44

Do you remember what the word *natural* means? He is referring to our soulish body. There is a soulish body and there is a spiritual body. Let's continue to look a little further in the succeeding verses: "Now this I say, brethren, that flesh and blood cannot inherit the kingdom of God; nor does corruption inherit incorruption" (verse 50). In other words, this body that we are used to is not going to be able to survive in God's Kingdom.

We have a wonderfully familiar illustration in our times from modern science. When we send people into space, even a few miles away from the earth's surface, they cannot survive unless they are in a special capsule that reproduces earth's atmosphere. The physical body is incapable of surviving out there.

This is even more applicable when it comes to the Kingdom of heaven. We are going to need more than a space capsule: We are going to need a totally different body. Paul says this: "Behold, I tell you a mystery: We shall not all sleep [in death], but we shall all be changed" (verse 51).

Can you make that declaration as you read these words again: *We shall all be changed . . .*

in a moment, in the twinkling of an eye, at the last trumpet. For the trumpet will sound, and the dead will be raised incorruptible, and we shall be changed. For this corruptible must put on incorruption, and this mortal must put on immortality. So when this corruptible [body] has put on incorruption, and this mortal [body] has put on immortality, then shall be brought to pass the saying that is written, "Death is swallowed up in victory."

verses 52–54

Death is our last enemy (see 1 Corinthians 15:26). Death's final defeat is still to come, because death is going to be cast into the lake of fire (see Revelation 20:14).

Have you ever realized that death is Satan's greatest triumph? He is proud of every death that takes place. He chalks that up as a victory for himself. But this passage testifies that his victory is going to be turned into defeat.

Five Changes in Our Bodies

I want to emphasize for you five changes mentioned by Paul, and quoted above, that will take place in your body. Let's focus carefully upon them, because they are not altogether easy to remember.

Change number one is from corruptible to incorruptible. *Corruptible* means "being subject to decay," and it defines our present bodies. Even if we never get sick, our bodies are still decaying. When you get to an older age, you will have a few wrinkles. Certain changes inevitably take place. But God intends to change your body from corruptible to incorruptible.

Change number two is from dishonor to glory.

Change number three is from weakness to power. Actually, power is more potent than strength, and glory is more exciting than honor.

127

Change number four is from soulish to spiritual. This has been a major focus for us in prior chapters. The soulish body should be subject to the spirit; the spirit has to work through the soul to activate the body. My belief is (and this is just my opinion) that in the resurrected body, the spirit will direct the body to do whatever it wants without having to go through the soul.

I do not know exactly what will happen to the soul, but let me add one interesting point to provide a possible answer. The soul, the life, is in the blood. See Leviticus 17:11, where "life" in Hebrew is *nephesh*, or "soul." Some people believe that we will have bloodless bodies. They contend that when Jesus rose from the dead, He had flesh and bone, but nothing is said about His blood. That is pure speculation, but it will be interesting to find out, won't it?

Finally, change number five is from mortal to immortal. That is exciting!

Why not take a moment here to proclaim those changes out loud: From corruptible to incorruptible. From dishonor to glory. From weakness to power. From soulish to spiritual. From mortal to immortal.

Don't you feel good when you say that? If not, I am sorry for you. Those words should inspire and excite us.

These changes we will experience are summed up at the end of Philippians 3, which is the portion of Scripture we began with in our previous chapter. Paul says,

> For our citizenship is in heaven, from which we also eagerly wait for the Savior, the Lord Jesus Christ, who will transform our lowly body that it may be conformed to His glorious body, according to the working by which He is able even to subdue all things to Himself.
>
> verses 20–21

Temporarily we may be residents of the United States or the Philippines or China or Japan or Canada, but that is not our permanent citizenship. Our permanent citizenship is in heaven. That is where we really belong. And Paul says it is from heaven that we are eagerly waiting for the Savior. Are you eagerly waiting? I hope you are.

Out of Humiliation into Glory

This translation of these verses from Philippians says that when Jesus comes, He is going to change our lowly bodies to be like His glorious body. What the Greek actually says is that He will change "the body of our humiliation, to be like the body of His glory."

We need to bear in mind that we are currently living in a body of humiliation. You realize that, don't you? Why is this true? Because we rebelled against God. As a result, He has ordained that we live in a body that continually reminds us we are being humiliated.

Here is an everyday example. It does not matter how rich you are. You can dine on the most expensive and well-prepared food. You can drink the most delicious drinks. But you know perfectly well you are going to have to go to the bathroom.

Let me ask you a rather stark question. Has anybody ever been dignified in the bathroom? So every time you visit the restroom, you are reminded you are in a body of humiliation.

In the same vein, you can dress in the most elegant clothes, perfume yourself, do your hair up. But if you have to walk fast in hot weather because you are a little bit late, what happens? If you are a more dignified kind of person, you begin to perspire. If you are just the normal kind of person, you sweat. Once again you are reminded you are in a body of humiliation.

It is a good thing for us to be reminded. I believe a lot of contemporary culture is really trying to evade that issue. Some

129

of us try to arrange ourselves in such a way as not to be reminded of the humiliation of our bodies. But we cannot do it. The good news of Scripture is that we are going to be changed. We will get a body like His. He alone can change us.

First John 3 describes the moment we will be changed:

> Beloved, now we are children of God; and it has not yet been revealed what we shall be, but we know that when He is revealed [when we see Him with our eyes], we shall be like Him, for we shall see Him as He is.
>
> 1 John 3:2

This is the moment we will be changed. When we see our Lord Jesus Christ with our own eyes we will be changed instantly.

Our Highest Motivation

I believe the excited anticipation of the Lord's return is an essential part of New Testament Christianity. Our Christianity is not in harmony with the New Testament if we are not excitedly expecting the Lord to come back.

Let me quickly give you some Scriptures in the words of Paul that highlight this anticipation. First is 1 Corinthians 1:7. In the middle of a sentence, as Paul is writing to the Corinthian church, he says, "Come short in no gift [*charisma*], eagerly waiting for the revelation of our Lord Jesus Christ."

Paul expected the Corinthians to be eagerly waiting for the revelation in glory of the Lord Jesus Christ. Incidentally, this verse is pretty good evidence that God did not intend to withdraw the charismatic gifts. Paul is saying, "I want you to be lacking in no charismatic gift as you eagerly wait for the coming of the Lord."

In Titus 2:11–12 Paul says,

> For the grace of God that brings salvation has appeared to all men, teaching us that, denying ungodliness and worldly lusts, we should live soberly, righteously, and godly in the present age.

Why should we live soberly, righteously and godly? What is our motivation for living in a holy way right now? The next verse tells us. It is because we are "looking for the blessed hope and glorious appearing of our great God and Savior Jesus Christ" (verse 13). We are waiting, looking for His return.

Notice in this verse that not only is Jesus our Savior, He is also the great God. If you have any difficulty saying that Jesus is God, you have a significant problem. Scripture tells us plainly that He is our great God and our Savior.

Then in 2 Timothy 4:7–8, Paul says,

> I have fought the good fight, I have finished the race, I have kept the faith. Finally, there is laid up for me the crown of righteousness, which the Lord, the righteous Judge, will give to me on that Day, and not to me only but also to all who have loved His appearing.

There is a crown—a special crown—for those who have loved His appearing. The Greek word for *love* here is the same word from which we get *agape*. It is a very strong, active word. The New International Version translates this as "those who long for his appearing." God has His eye on those who are longing for the appearing of Jesus.

Then in Hebrews 9:27, we read: "It is appointed for men to die once, but after this the judgment." There are two appointments we will not miss. We might miss every appointment on earth, but we will be in attendance for death and judgment.

Continuing in Hebrews we read: "So Christ was offered once to bear the sins of many. To those who eagerly wait for Him He will appear a second time, apart from sin, for salvation" (verse 28).

To whom will He appear? To those who eagerly wait for Him.

I want to make a suggestion to you. This is something you can check for yourself. As we have seen in the Scriptures above, the excited anticipation of the Lord's return is the main motive given in the New Testament for holy living. In fact, almost every place where Scripture speaks about holiness, it is linked to the Lord's return.

My conclusion is that if the Church is not confronted regularly with the expectation of the Lord's return, the level of holiness in the Church will be lower than it ought to be. Is that logical? And is it true to experience?

Dear friend, I do not think we have any idea of how far the Church is below the standard of God's holiness. I once heard about the experience of a participant in one of John Wimber's meetings during a time when they were praying for one another. She gave this prayer request: "I want to know how Jesus feels about the Church." So they prayed for her. After that, every time the word *Church* was mentioned, she burst into tears.

Are you waiting eagerly for Him? If you are, take a moment to thank the Lord.

Out of Time; Into Eternity

I hear critics say over and over again that the early Church was wrong in expecting the return of the Lord because He did not come. I would have to say that I would rather be wrong with the early Church and get the results they got, than be right with those theologians and get the results they get.

Frankly, I do not believe those critics are right. One of the interesting subjects that philosophers and physicists deal with is time. It is a very difficult subject. I have suggested to you within this text that at death your spirit and your soul, the nonmaterial parts of you, will go to heaven. Your body will be consigned in some way or another to the grave. When you pass out of time into heaven, you pass out of time into eternity. Time no longer applies. That is hard for the human mind to understand.

But here is the interesting fact. Physicists have computed that if you could get into a spacecraft and travel with tremendous speed—say you go off to some distant star and come back in two weeks—you would feel that two weeks have elapsed. But when you step out of the spacecraft back on earth, you would find that three successive generations on earth had been born. That much time would have elapsed on earth. What is the point we need to understand? Time is complicated.

What I am trying to say is that after death, time is no longer. The question of whether or not someone has been dead for some two thousand years does not matter. That time frame may be true in the earthly sense, but it is not true in the eternal sense.

When I lie down in death and my eyes close, and my spirit and soul pass out of time, what is the next event in time that is going to happen to me as a true believer? The resurrection. And when these eyes of mine open again, what is the first thing I'm going to see? The Lord. So those early believers were not wrong, were they? The coming of the Lord is no farther away than your death in time. Do you follow that?

The Challenge for Us

As I close this chapter, I want to point out that I am issuing a challenge to holiness—and it is a much needed challenge for us.

I posed the question earlier in the book of whether or not you had any ideas of what it would mean for your body to be "preserved blameless" at the coming of the Lord.

> Now may the God of peace Himself sanctify you completely; and may your whole spirit, soul, and body be preserved blameless at the coming of our Lord Jesus Christ. He who calls you is faithful, who also will do it.
>
> 1 Thessalonians 5:23–24

I want to offer you these two thoughts to ponder.

First of all, your body is sanctified by the altar on which you have laid it. Scripture requires us to present our bodies to God as sacrifices on His altar. That altar sanctifies the offering. This means that your body, in all of its humiliation, can be sanctified because you have presented it to the Lord.

Second, we are required to yield every member to the Lord for His service. If you have sincerely presented your whole body to the Lord, you have taken your hands off. You have said, "God, it's Your body. Do with it what You want." If you have sincerely committed every member to the Lord for Him to control, you have come a very long way.

13

You Are the Treasure

O afflicted one, storm-tossed, and not comforted,
Behold, I will set your stones in antimony,
And your foundations I will lay in sapphires.
Moreover, I will make your battlements of rubies,
And your gates of crystal,
And your entire wall of precious stones.
All your sons will be taught of the LORD;
And the well-being of your sons will be great.
In righteousness you will be established;
You will be far from oppression, for you will
     not fear;
And from terror, for it will not come near you.

Isaiah 54:11–14, NASB

We have looked at the amazing way God has formed us and destined us—spirit, soul and body—to fulfill His purposes for us. No matter how far we may seem from His ideal, we must remember that God has never given up on that breath that He breathed into that body of clay. Ultimately He sent Jesus to bring it back to Himself.

Scripture says that *Jesus came to seek and to save that which was lost and cut off.* That is why He came. He came for the descendants of Adam. Such is His love for us.

Jesus' favorite title, which occurs more than eighty times in the gospels, is "the Son of Man." He was the Son of David, the Son of Abraham, but He called Himself the Son of Man, the Son of Adam, the representative of the Adamic race.

Now here is an amazing truth. First Timothy 2:5 says, "For there is one God and one Mediator between God and men, the Man Christ Jesus." This was written many years after the death and resurrection of Jesus. It reveals that a Man sits on the throne of God: the Man, Christ Jesus. That is a breathtaking thought if we can absorb it.

A representative of our race has taken His seat at the highest place in the universe. A Man, Christ Jesus, is on the throne of God. You see, God takes the lowest and raises it to the highest. He started with dust, but His destiny is to end on the throne.

That is how valuable we are in the sight of God.

I would like to conclude our study by looking at a few verses from Matthew 13. Have you ever pondered this chapter? It is the chapter of the seven parables. It is a rich and exciting chapter. I want to take two of the shortest parables. One of these is just one verse and the other is two verses. Think about your true identity as you read.

The Hidden Treasure

My Bible gives this heading to the first one: "The Parable of the Hidden Treasure." Jesus is speaking: "Again, the kingdom of heaven is like treasure hidden in a field, which a man found and hid; and for joy over it he goes and sells all that he has and buys that field" (Matthew 13:44).

If you think in terms of the history of the Middle East, how do you imagine that treasure got hidden in the field? Well, probably an invading army marched through at some time. A man who was afraid of losing his possessions went quickly into his field and buried his treasure. But who knows what might have happened next? War may have swept into the region and carried him away forever. He never got back, and the treasure lay buried in the field.

Years later, another man comes along and discovers the treasure. Let's say that this man is very crafty. He does not tell anybody about it. He hides it. He covers it up. And then he goes and buys the field as though it is just an ordinary piece of property. Maybe he even pays a slightly excessive price.

People marvel, "Why would he buy that field? There's nothing in that field. It's not worth what he paid for it." But once he owns the field, he digs up the treasure, you see. And then people understand why he bought it.

Understanding the Parable

I know there are different ways of interpreting parables, but I would like to give you the way I interpret this. And I want to say to you: That man who bought the field is Jesus. The field, the parables tell us, is the world. Jesus died for the whole world. He paid the price for the whole world. But it is not the world He wants: It is the treasure in the field. What is the treasure? God's people.

Jesus was willing to pay the price for an apparently worthless field in order to get the treasure, which is you and me. That is how much He cares for us. That is how much He thinks of us. That is how much we mean to Him. We are not unimportant; we are not insignificant; we are not worthless. We are extremely valuable. We are so valuable that Jesus gave His life to purchase us.

Be Glad to Be You

Never again should you talk about yourself as if you were unimportant or insignificant or worthless. Just discard all that thinking. It is not scriptural. Now, I am not telling you to be prideful, but I am telling you to realize your true value. You gain nothing by an attitude that proclaims, *I don't amount to much. I'm just a little something or other.* That is not pleasing to God. You are a son or a daughter of God. He has no second-class children. You are important. You are very, very valuable. You are special.

Begin to understand that as you read these words. Drop any sense of worthlessness. You do not have to apologize for being you. It is you that God wants. He wants you the way you are. But remember that you are not glorifying God if you are trying to be humble. That is not humility; it is actually unbelief.

Right now, you are a child of God if you have received Jesus by faith. You are part of the magnificent treasure.

Digging Out the Treasure

Regarding this parable, I believe that the ministry of the Gospel is digging the treasure out. Jesus bought the field, but He leaves it to us to dig up the treasure. When treasure has been under the earth for a long while, it is often corrupted and tarnished. That is part of the ministry, too. It is to polish it up and clean it up. I believe that is the ministry God has given me—to polish up the treasure that has been so long under the ground. God has given me a sense of the value of God's people.

Exceedingly Precious

When I was a very new Christian, just about two years old in the Lord, I was in the medical corps of the British army. The army posted me to the Sudan.

Believe me when I say that the Sudan is a tough country. As a matter of fact, it is even tougher now. It is one of the most persecuting of all countries toward Christians at this time.

Originally, I went to Khartoum, which is the capital. Then the army posted me to a little, out of the way railway station town called Atbara. As I traveled there by train, being a British soldier I was in a compartment in which no local people were admitted. I was not responsible for it, and I considered that rather unfair treatment, but that's the way it was.

We got to this station, somewhere north of Khartoum, and I looked out on the platform—it was just a sea of living beings. Men, women, old men, children, babies, donkeys, mules, camels, chickens, everything.

And quite without planning it, I said to myself *I wonder what God thinks of all these people.* I received an immediate answer, which I certainly was not expecting. This is the answer He gave me: *Some weak, some foolish, some proud, some wicked and some exceedingly precious.* That's how God views humanity. Some are weak, some are foolish, some are proud and some are wicked, but in the midst of them all there are those who are exceedingly precious.

Once I arrived in Atbara, I was put in charge of what is called in the medical language of the army a "reception station."

Actually, it was like being in a palace. I had two rooms and two beds with nobody in them. I had a nightshirt for the first time. For two or three years I had slept in my underwear. At that time, I had no patients in the reception station, so I put on one of the nightshirts and slept in one of the beds.

At some point in the middle of the night, I got a tremendous supernatural burden of prayer for the people of the Sudan. I tell you honestly, they are not easy people to love. They are pretty fierce, and they are not gracious or easy to make a connection with.

139

But that night, in the middle of the night, I got up. I was so burdened with prayer that I was pacing to and fro in that little room in my white flannel nightshirt. As I was praying for the souls of the people of the Sudan I looked down at my nightshirt, and I have to tell you it was luminous. There was such a sense of the glory of God that my nightshirt was actually shining. (In that moment, God gave me a little glimpse of how He values intercession.)

Sometime later, I was moved to another station on the Red Sea called Jubayt. There I was put in charge of another facility. Now I was only a corporal. I could not achieve any higher rank because I had declared myself to be a conscientious objector. At that location, I was put in charge of the native labor—the Sudani labor—in a hospital. I had to deal with the head man of the Sudani labor forces, whose name was Ali. We had to meet every morning in my office and plan the activities for the day.

Frankly, I could not see any way to relate to Ali. He was distant to me, and I was distant to him.

Making a Connection

Then one day as we talked, I discovered that Ali believed in Satan. So I told him, "I believe in Satan, too." As strange as it may seem, that was the first connection between us. We both believed in Satan.

One day he was late in reporting to my office, and he came in limping. He said, "I've been to the reception station because I have something on my foot that is hurting me." By then I had read in the Bible how healing prayer is offered—though I do not think I had ever seen anybody lay hands on people and pray for them. If I had, I did not remember it. But I knew it was in the Bible. So I asked, "Would you like me to pray for you?" Ali said he would.

Well, I treated him like a bomb that was about to explode.
I stood at a careful distance, put my hands on him and prayed
a simple prayer. That was all I could do. About a week later,
he came in and showed me his foot. It was completely healed.
After that, we had a connection. We became friends.

Bonding with Ali

In the days that followed, Ali wanted to teach me how to
ride a camel, so I learned to ride a camel. Believe me when
I report that riding a camel is no joke. I do not know what
it is about a camel, but when one part is going up, another
is going down. You never have a stable ride. I am not talking about the camels that they turn loose at the pyramids in
Egypt. Those are not Sudani camels.

As Ali and I grew closer, I asked him, "Would you like me
to read to you from the Bible?"

He said yes. He was getting interested. So I thought we
would start at John's gospel. I read from the King James
Version, which is the only version that most people used in
those days. All the English that Ali had learned was from
soldiers. He could not read or write, but he had a very accurate memory.

So I read the King James Version, translating it into soldier's English all the way, which was quite a challenge.

A short time afterward, Ali said, "Why don't we take a
ride on our camels and go out somewhere?"

I said, "Fine."

I was in charge of the rations, so we armed ourselves with
all we needed to eat. We rode out on our two camels and
sat down at the bottom of a hill. A little stream of brackish
water was running down the hill. Now, I am not sure that
I would do today what I did then, and I am not necessarily
recommending it, but this is what happened.

Ali said, "Now, we [Sudanis] drink this water. But you white people, you don't drink this water."

"Well," I said, "since there's nothing else to drink, I'll drink it."

"Why would you do that?"

And I replied, "Well, Jesus said if you drink any deadly thing it will not hurt you."

So I drank the water. And he drank the water. And we both did well.

A New Birth

During that outing, we did some more reading together. I read from the gospel of John about being born again. That phrase lodged in his mind—*born again, born again.*

When we were on our camels on the way back, he said, "Born again. What's that?"

"Well," I said, "God will give you a new heart."

Ali just laughed—because in those days heart transplants did not exist. He could not understand anything about a new heart.

"It means," I said, "that you get the life of God." Then I asked, "Would you like to be born again?"

He said that he would.

"This evening," I said, "when the sun sets, you go to your hut and I'll go to my billet. You pray to be born again, and I'll pray for you."

So he said, "All right."

When we met the next morning, I looked at him and asked, "Did you pray?"

"Yes."

"Did you get anything?"

"No."

I was disappointed. But the Holy Spirit whispered in my ear, *Remember, he's a Muslim.* That thought prompted me to ask Ali another question: "Did you pray in the name of Jesus?"

"No," he replied.

"Oh, you have to pray in the name of Jesus if you want to be born again. Are you willing to do that?"

"Yes."

"Well," I said, "this evening you go to your hut and I'll go to my billet. We'll pray again."

When I met him the next morning, I looked at him and said, "You got it!"

He said, "Yes, I did."

Everybody in the hospital heard about the change that took place in Ali's life. They came to me and said, "What happened to your friend Ali?"

I said, "He got born again."

They said, "What's that?"

And I said, "Let me tell you!"

The commanding officer of the hospital sent for me and said, "What happened to your friend Ali?"

I said, "He got born again."

This officer was a Presbyterian—a good, religious man. But he did not know anything about the new birth. So as a result of Ali's experience, two of my fellow soldiers came to the Lord.

I want to say simply that all of those results came out of that night of intense intercession for the people of the Sudan. Scripture tells us that without travail there will be no birth. Unless we travail in prayer, we won't see any birth. Isaiah 66:8 says, "As soon as Zion travailed, she brought forth her children" (ASV). As soon as the Church travails, she will begin to bring forth children.

The Merchant and the Pearl

This next parable is one I dearly love: "Again, the kingdom of heaven is like a merchant seeking beautiful pearls, who, when he had found one pearl of great price, went and sold all that he had and bought it" (Matthew 13:45–46).

There are different ways of applying this passage, but I want to give you one application that can make a change in your life. First of all, I want to point out that the man in this parable was a merchant. He was not a tourist. He was a man who spent all his life dealing in pearls, and he knew the real value of a pearl. When he found this one pearl, so wonderful and so precious, he sold all that he had to buy it.

This is a little modern interpretation of that parable. I can imagine the man going home to his wife and saying, "Honey, I've sold our car."

"You sold our car? Why did you do that?"

"Well, I found a pearl."

"A pearl? One pearl?"

"Yes."

"Well, thank God at any rate we still have a roof over our heads."

"No, I sold our house, too!"

You see, this was a man who knew what things were worth. He found one pearl that was worth more than everything he had in life. And he sold it all and bought the pearl.

Now, I want you to think for a moment. Think of yourself as being that one pearl—that uniquely beautiful and valuable pearl.

You know that pearls are formed as the result of a process of suffering. Out of the irritation caused to an oyster by one grain of sand, a pearl comes forth. Maybe you have been through suffering. Maybe you have begun to question whether God really loves you. Maybe you have begun to think, *I'm not really worth much. I'm not important to God. There are other people who are important, but I'm not.*

I want to tell you, that is not true. You are important to God. So important to God that He gave His Son, Jesus, to die on the cross for you. You. Specifically you.

Jesus sold all that He had. He left all the riches of glory in heaven, became a carpenter's son, became a traveling preacher. When He died on the cross, He literally owned nothing! He was buried in a borrowed linen cloth in a borrowed tomb. "You know the grace of our Lord Jesus Christ," Paul says, "that though He was rich, yet for your sakes He became poor, that you through His poverty might become rich" (2 Corinthians 8:9). Jesus sold all that He had. He gave up everything for you.

I know that He purchased the treasure in the field. That is God's people as a company. But He also purchased the one pearl of great price, which is you.

You.

You, in your weaknesses, your failures, your lack of understanding, your frustrations, your loneliness, your fears. Jesus died for *you.*

I really believe—I am utterly convinced of this—that if no one else would ever have gotten saved, Jesus would have died for me. If there had never been anybody else—and thank God, there are millions of others—Jesus would have given His all for me.

I like to make His love individual. I like to make it personal. I like to say, "*For me,* He died. *For me,* He gave up His throne. *For me,* He laid down His life. *For me,* He suffered on the cross, and He was buried. And then, *for me,* He rose, He ascended, and He is at the Father's right hand."

If you have a problem with self-worth, if you have a low sense of self-esteem, if you do not really feel that you matter very much to God or to others, this truth is for you. You may be lonely, you may be wondering how you ever got here to the

145

point of reading this. I want to tell you God brought you to this point. You have an appointment with God right now.

Think of yourself this way. Think of that merchant who has bought the pearl. He is holding it in the palm of his hand, looking down at it. He is saying, "You're beautiful. You're the most beautiful one I have ever seen. You cost me everything I had, but you were worth it. You are so beautiful."

Now I want you to realize that you, individually, are that pearl. You, yourself. You are there in the palm of the Lord's hand. He is looking down at you and saying, "You're so beautiful. You cost Me all I had, but I love you. I'm glad I died for you."

A Prayer of Affirmation

As we close this book, I want to help you a little further, because I know from dealing with people how deep this problem of a low sense of self-esteem can go. I want to suggest an action to you if you have a problem believing that you are really valuable to God. I want you to take a decisive step and follow me as I lead you in a specific prayer. If you have a problem with self-esteem, do not be afraid and do not be ashamed. Just pray the prayer that I am about to give you.

This is a very important and solemn moment. The devil did everything he could to prevent me from bringing this teaching to you, but he is a defeated enemy.

Right now I want you to think of yourself as that pearl of great price. For a little while, shut everything else out and see yourself as the one pearl in the palm of the hand of Jesus. And remember those hands bear the scars of His sufferings.

I want you to listen as Jesus is speaking to you. He is saying, "You're beautiful. You cost Me all I had, but you're worth it. I'm glad I gave My life for *you*."

Can you say these next words with that picture in your mind? Please pray the prayer that appears in the paragraphs below:

> Lord Jesus, I thank You that You died for me. That You gave Yourself on the cross, a death of agony and shame to purchase me.
>
> And, Lord, I belong to You. I am Yours forever. I know You will never leave me. You will never forsake me. I am etched upon the palm of Your hand.
>
> I am beautiful in Your eyes. More beautiful than all the worlds You created, because You set Your love on me. And because You love me, Lord, I love You.
>
> Receive my love as I give it to You now. I give myself afresh to You right now. I thank You that I'm not unwanted. I'm not unworthy. I'm not a castoff. I'm not rejected. I am accepted in the Beloved—in You, Lord Jesus. I am accepted. Thank You, thank You, thank You again and again! Thank You for that wonderful love that You poured out on the cross. Thank You, Lord.

If you have prayed that prayer just now, I want you to take one more step in the next few days. I want you to seek out someone who is close to you. Go to that person and tell him or her what you have prayed. That one may need to hear it and pray it as well. I want you to look that person right in the eye and say, "I'm not rejected. I'm not unwanted. I'm precious to the Lord." Will you do that?

As I close this book, I want you to verbalize this wonderful truth one more time. Please say it once again: "I'm not rejected. I'm not unwanted. I am precious to the Lord."

A Prayer of Sanctification

We have several times turned to 1 Thessalonians 5:23 as one of the key Scriptures for understanding who we are and where we are headed. This is a prayer that the apostle Paul prayed for Christians, for the Body of Christ. He prayed specifically

147

for the Christians in Thessalonica, but obviously his prayer is for all of us.

Over the years, I have found it very helpful to take a relevant passage of Scripture and make it a confession or a prayer. In fact, Ruth and I make the confession personal, like this: "Now may the God of peace Himself sanctify us completely, and may our whole spirit, soul and body be preserved blameless at the coming of our Lord Jesus Christ."

I would like to invite you now to say that as your personal prayer. It can be very meaningful for you, believing that God will begin to answer that prayer for you.

You probably know that the word *sanctify* means "to make holy." In this prayer you are going to be praying to God to make you holy. As I have stated, if there is one desperate need of the Body of Christ today, I would say it is the need for holiness. So this is a very relevant prayer.

Why not go ahead and say it now, phrase by phrase. Are you ready?

> Now may the God of peace Himself sanctify me completely, and may my whole spirit, soul and body be preserved blameless at the coming of our Lord Jesus Christ.

If you prayed both of these prayers, you have not only affirmed God's acceptance, but also asked Him to prepare you—spirit, soul and body—to be completely His. And that is a prayer that He will always answer.

Do you realize how valuable you are? I trust that in the pages of this book I have given you some basis for an answer. The implications of our identity in the eyes of God are staggering. May you grow daily in the knowledge—and joy—of how much you matter to Him.

Index

joy, 48–50
Judaism, 117
judgment, 131

king of Tyre, 13
King's College (Cambridge), 30
knowledge, 73, 96

Lazarus, 112, 119
likeness of God, 14–15, 36, 108
love, 131
Lucifer, 12–14. See also Satan
lust, 57

man
    creation of, 14–19
    destiny of, 18, 35–36
    paradox of, 34–36
    triune nature of, 15, 36, 39, 83, 108
manipulation, 100
Marx, Karl, 24
Mary Magdalene, 112
men, abdication of responsibility, 22
merchant and the pearl, parable of,
    144–46
Messiah, 117
mind, 44, 73–74, 84, 102
mirror, God's Word as, 33–34
mistrust, 36
money, 27
motivation, 130–32
Mount of Olives, 118

napach, 17
Nashville, 100
natural body, 95
natural man, 96
nephesh, 128
new birth, 40, 46, 109, 142–43
new creation, 61, 106–7
new personality, 64–65
Nicodemus, 62

old age, 109
"old man, the," 54

pain, 48
paraclete, 116
Paul, 107
    on charismatic gifts, 130
    on faith, 67
    on faithfulness of God, 91
    on God-consciousness, 42
    on human personality, 37
    on joy, 49
    on new creation, 106–7
    on rebellion, 56
    on the resurrection, 114–16, 120,
        126
    on the Spirit of Christ, 64
    on spiritual death, 55
    on transformation of the body, 128
peace, 76
personality. See human personality
Philip, and Ethiopian eunuch, 122
philosophy, 30, 76, 132
physical death, 57
physics, 132–33
Plato, 102
pleasure, 48
pneuma, 41, 94
pneumatikos, 94
pneumatology, 40
power, 127
praise, 99
prayer, 72, 99
    of affirmation, 146–47
    of sanctification, 147–48
preached Word, 64
pride, 12–14, 27, 97, 138
Prince, Derek
    books by, 9–10
    tenderness of, 7–8
Prince, Lydia, 47–48
psuche, 41, 45
psuchekos, 94
psychiatry, 96
psychology, 33, 72, 96

Derek Prince (1915–2003) was born in India of British parents. He was educated as a scholar of Greek and Latin at Eton College and King's College, Cambridge, in England. Upon graduation he held a fellowship (equivalent to a professorship) in ancient and modern philosophy at King's College. He also studied Hebrew, Aramaic and modern languages at Cambridge and the Hebrew University in Jerusalem. As a student, he was a philosopher and self-proclaimed agnostic.

While in the British Medical Corps during World War II, Derek began to study the Bible as a philosophical work. Converted through a powerful encounter with Jesus Christ, he was baptized in the Holy Spirit a few days later. Out of this encounter, he formed two conclusions: first, that Jesus Christ is alive; second, that the Bible is a true, relevant, up-to-date book. These conclusions altered the whole course of his life, which he then devoted to studying and teaching the Bible as the Word of God.

Discharged from the army in Jerusalem in 1945, he married Lydia Christensen, founder of a children's home there. Upon their marriage, he immediately became father to Lydia's eight adopted daughters—six Jewish, one Palestinian Arab and one English. Together, the family saw the rebirth of the state of Israel in 1948. In the late 1950s, they adopted another daughter while Derek was serving as principal of a teacher training college in Kenya.

In 1963, the Princes immigrated to the United States and pastored a church in Seattle. In 1973, Derek became one of the founders of Intercessors for America. His book *Shaping History through Prayer and Fasting* has awakened Christians around the world to their responsibility to pray for their governments. Many consider underground translations of the book as instrumental in the fall of Communist regimes in the USSR, East Germany and Czechoslovakia.

Lydia Prince died in 1975, and Derek married Ruth Baker (a single mother to three adopted children) in 1978. He met his second wife, like his first wife, while she was serving the Lord in Jerusalem. Ruth died in December 1998 in Jerusalem, where they had lived since 1981.

Until a few years before his own death in 2003 at the age of 88, Derek persisted in the ministry God had called him to as he traveled the world, imparting God's revealed truth, praying for the sick and afflicted and sharing his prophetic insights into world events in the light of Scripture. Internationally recognized as a Bible scholar and spiritual patriarch, he established a teaching ministry that spanned six continents and more than sixty years. He is the author of more than fifty books, six hundred audio teachings and one hundred video teachings, many of which have been translated and published in more than one hundred languages. He pioneered teaching on such groundbreaking themes as generational curses, the biblical significance of Israel and demonology.

Derek's radio program, which began in 1979, has been translated into more than a dozen languages and continues to touch lives. His main gift of explaining the Bible and its teaching in a clear and simple way has helped build a foundation of faith in millions of lives. Derek's nondenominational, nonsectarian approach has made his teaching equally relevant and helpful to people from all racial and religious backgrounds, and his teaching is estimated to have reached more than half the globe.

In 2002, Derek said, "It is my desire—and I believe the Lord's desire—that this ministry continue the work, which God began through me more than sixty years ago, until Jesus returns."

Derek Prince Ministries continues to distribute his teachings and to train missionaries, church leaders and congregations through the outreaches of more than thirty DPM offices around the world, including primary work in Australia, Canada, China, France, Germany, the Netherlands, New Zealand, Norway, Russia, South Africa, Switzerland, the United Kingdom and the United States. For current information about these and other worldwide locations, visit www.derekprince.com.

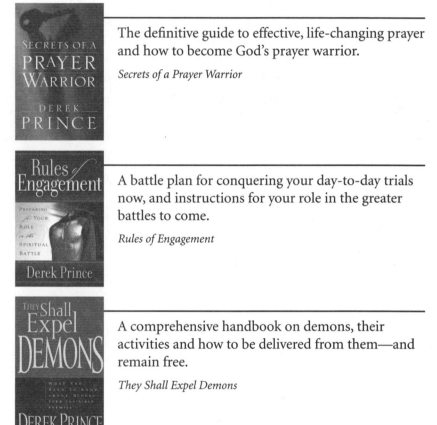